Connor Court Quarterly, Volume 14

INTELLIGENT DESIGN
INTERVIEW WITH BILL DEMBSKI

DEFENDING THE EMBATTLED CHRISTIAN HERITAGE OF WESTERN CIVILIZATION, CAMPION COLLEGE
Paul Morrissey

SHERIDAN COLLEGE
Augusto Zimmermann

Published by Connor Court Publishing Pty Ltd, 2020.

Copyright © As a collection, Connor Court Publishing.

CONNOR COURT PUBLISHING PTY LTD
PO Box 7257
Redland Bay QLD 4165
sales@connorcourt.com
www.connorcourtpublishing.com.au

ISBN: (pbk.) 9781922449733

Cover design by Ian James.

Printed in Australia.

PREVIOUS ISSUE OF

THE CONNOR COURT QUARTERLY

Connor Court Quarterly, Volume 13

- Our Ten Days that Shook the World -- Jeffrey Tucker
- Nicola Roxon, How Smart You Were -- Marc Hendrickx
- An Egregious Statistical Horror Story Suffused with Incense and Lugubrious Accents -- Jeffrey Tucker
- Why Australia Needs Equality Of Sacrifice -- Daniel Wild

www.connorcourtpublishing.com.au

INTELLIGENT DESIGN

Interview of Bill Dembski

This interview, originally given back in 2012 and then revised in 2016, appeared on the educational website TheBestSchools.org. Bill's good friend and colleague James Barham conducted the interview. The interview, updated again in August 2019 and May 2021, appears here at Bill Dembski.com. listed articles in In *The Design Inference: Eliminating Chance Through Small Probabilities* (Cambridge University Press, 1998), the first book on intelligent design published by a major university press, he analyzed the connections linking chance, probability, and intelligent causation.

In 2000, he founded the first intelligent design thinktank at a research university, Baylor's Michael Polanyi Center. As a design theorist, he has lectured widely on intelligent design, appearing on numerous radio and television programs, including ABC's Nightline and Jon Stewart's The Daily Show.

James Barham: Thank you for this interview. You wear many hats, and keep putting on new ones, most recently as an educational reformer. You are a mathematician, philosopher, theologian, and prolific author. Even though officially retired from intelligent design, you remain one of its leading lights. The intelligent design (ID) movement has mounted a very public and highly controversial attack on mainstream neo-Darwinian evolutionary theory, and its impact continues to be felt. So we have a lot of ground to cover.

Let's begin by asking you for some personal background. Where were you born and raised? Were you brought up in an academic environment? What set you on the track toward a life of scholarship, writing, and teaching?

Early Days

Bill Dembski: Thanks for the opportunity to do this interview, which looks to remain my most extensive interview to date. I was born on July 18, 1960, in Chicago (St. Mary of Nazareth Hospital in the Bucktown neighborhood). My dad, who was from Chicago, was a World War II veteran who had dropped out of high school, but after the war finished it in an accelerated program on the GI Bill. He then went on to study at the University of Illinois at Champaign-Urbana.

Though from a thoroughly blue-collar background (he was selling newspapers on the streets of Chicago at age seven—those were Depression-era days and his father had abandoned the family), he came to love the academic life. After getting his bachelor's in biology, he went on for a master's in biology and another in education, all at the University of Illinois.

After that, in the early to mid-1950s, he was teaching high school in the Chicago area.

He was still single and he loved teaching biology, so in 1957 he went on a Fulbright scholarship to Germany. There he met my mother (who was a German citizen).

They got married in 1958 and moved to the U.S. in 1959. Upon their return, my dad started teaching biology at the University of Illinois, Navy Pier campus (which eventually became the University of Illinois at Chicago Circle and then—as it is today—the University of Illinois at Chicago).

Although it was not mandatory to have a Ph.D. back then to teach at the college level, as it is now, his supervisors at the University of Illinois encouraged him to get one. It turned out that getting that degree in the U.S. would have required a lot of jumping through hoops, so he decided to return to Germany and get his doctorate there (from the University of Erlangen—Erlangen being the town where he and my mother had met). In Europe, doctoral level work tends to focus directly on research rather than requiring lots of course work, qualifying exams, and other preparation (which in my dad's case, with already two master's degrees, would have constituted busy work).

My dad was 40 when he started his doctorate in Germany in 1963, and it took him three years to complete it. My parents had saved up $10,000 during the three years prior to that. During those three years before leaving for Erlangen, we typically lived on 50 cents a day for food (I don't remember, but so I'm told). We also didn't have a car, with my dad taking public transportation to work every day in Chicago.

Once in Germany, my parents carefully apportioned their money. I was three when we arrived (I had no siblings). My parents immediately bought a gray Volkswagen bug, which we drove the three years that we were there. It's incredible to think that $10,000 could cover a family of three for three years as my dad worked full-time on his doctorate. Sure, the exchange rate of the DM (deutsch mark) to the $US (US dollar) was great back then (four to one), but even accounting for inflation, it's still hard to fathom.

When our family returned to the U.S. in 1967, the country was a very different place. The University of Illinois, though having encouraged my dad to get a PhD, did not hire him back—by "unfortunate coincidence," as they put it, his job had gone to a young Ph.D. from Harvard. So my dad taught for the City Colleges of Chicago. The campus where he taught had a lot of racial tension, with faculty getting mugged and even killed. Martin Luther King was assassinated during that time. The Black Panthers, with their berets and 50-caliber bullets around their necks, disrupted faculty meetings and forced the school president to resign. When my dad didn't return home at the expected hour, I recall my mother comforting me with the thought that if he got killed, at least I still had her. I remember the race riots and seeing Madison Avenue burning from our high-rise apartment in Uptown.

With my dad teaching for the City Colleges of Chicago, I saw first-hand the dark side of academic politics, the self-servingness of teacher unions, and the decay of learning standards. I also saw my dad's love for teaching and research wither. It didn't totally die because of his love for students and the satisfaction of seeing minds open up even despite the best efforts of a corrupt administration and misshapen philosophy of education to undermine learning. But I witnessed it all first hand, and it gave me a bad taste for aspects of the academy and probably more than anything contributed to my unwillingness to sacrifice intellectual work to academic fashion (for which I've paid a cost).

Despite my ambivalence toward the academy, it's always been front and center in my life. I always felt most at home in the world of discussion and ideas. And I always did well in the academy (until I fell a foul of it for questioning Darwinism). A life of scholarship, teaching, and writing therefore seemed to me inevitable from the start. How it's all played out has proved less inevitable.

When this interview was first conducted in January 2012 and then revised in May 2016, my parents were still alive. Since then both died, my dad in 2017 and my mom in 2018.

Religious Upbringing

JB: What religious tradition were you raised in? Was there ever a time in your life when you doubted the existence of God? Your conversion to Christianity occurred when you were a young adult. What was the backdrop for your conversion?

BD: I was raised a nominal Roman Catholic, with strong emphasis on the word "nominal." I jumped the required hoops at the appointed times (getting my first holy communion at age seven and being confirmed at age 13). We went to mass very sporadically. I rejected many of the standard doctrines, such as the deity of Christ and the reality of hell (I don't recall what I thought of Christ's resurrection, though I know I didn't dismiss it outright).

I went to public schools through the start of grade seven. Fourth through seventh grade was in the Evanston school system, which was nationally regarded as outstanding (Evanston Township High School was at the time regarded one of the best public high schools in the nation). Nonetheless, by the time I showed up, a permissive and secular educational philosophy had thoroughly undercut that school system.

Discipline was terrible. I was constantly being assaulted and getting into fights that I did not start. I remember being chased during recess outside by a boy with a baseball bat who meant to use it on me. When he threw it at me, I tried to get my hands on it and I meant to use it on him, I was so angry. My hands fumbled and I couldn't get a grip on it, so I just ran inside the building. Looking back, I think it was the grace of God that I didn't beat his head in.

On another occasion, I remember one boy waiting outside the school to beat me up, with about ten of his companions waiting eagerly to enjoy the festivities. They were all outside in clear view with clear intent. The assistant principal happened to be there. I pointed out to him all the boys standing around and that they meant to do me harm. Rather than take action, he simply shooed me to the door. I was totally disgusted. Rather than go out that way, I went to the very rear of the school and walked the long way home. There were many more incidents like this.

Yet, despite this bullying, my parents wouldn't pull me out of the school system. My dad, as I mentioned, was from a thoroughly blue-collar background. The best he offered me here was advice on how to fight and defend myself. He also spoke with the school administration on my behalf, but that made no difference. What finally caused my parents to pull me from the school was a disintegration of the curriculum in the seventh grade.

My parents went to an open house at the junior high school. In the science classroom, the word "pseudopodia" was misspelled on a large sign stuck to the blackboard. When my dad inquired, he found that the science teacher had misspelled it (big mistake, given that my dad was a biology professor!). In the math class, there was no textbook or clear course of study. When my dad asked what we were covering, the teacher waved his hands.

I still remember that math class. An A for the fall term could be gotten by computing 60 factorial by hand (this was in 1972 before calculators), which is 1 times 2 times 3 etc. all the way to 60—an 80 digit number. This was sheer busy work. It was on coming back from that open house that my parents pulled me from the public school system and sent me to Catholic schools.

I give this background, because it helps explain some of my contrarian ways. I came to loathe the permissive and secular philosophy that I saw as responsible for the utter nonsense I had to endure in the Evanston school system, the same philosophy that provides such a cozy home for Darwinian naturalism.

In any case, one might think that, upon entering Catholic schools, I would have been indoctrinated into this form of Christianity. But it didn't happen. I was a thoughtful kid and I had serious religious questions.

The nuns at Hardy Prep in Chicago were not interested, it seemed, in answering those questions.

I remember, in preparation for confirmation in the eighth grade, that I had to write a letter to the bishop. It was to be a *proforma* thank-you letter, but in it I raised some questions about confirmation, indicated that I really didn't understand what it was all about, and mused that one day I would (which I do now). The nun in charge sent the letter back and had me omit all this questioning, turning the letter into pabulum. Nor did she take me aside to answer my questions.

High school at Portsmouth Abbey, a prep school in Rhode Island, was better, but by then I had veered into Eastern philosophy and what later came to be called the New Age. When I left high school after three years to go to the University of Chicago, I recall being asked in a questionnaire for my religious preference. I put down Hindu.

It sounds crazy in hindsight, but religiously that's where I was. When I left Catholic school after my junior year, I had no intention of returning to Roman Catholicism, or to any form of Christianity for that matter. Christianity, it seemed to me, was completely lacking in power and relevance. I remember consciously closing the door on Christianity.

My parents never pushed religion on me. My mother always had an affection for Jesus—as a young girl, she seems to have had a divine encounter. But then in school, reading Hermann Hesse, she lost any traditional Christian belief. My dad would occasionally go to Catholic mass by himself—I think he found some comfort there. But there were a lot of secular elements to his thought. He was never a dogmatic Darwinist, but one of his favorite quotes was Robert Green Ingersoll's "In nature there are neither rewards nor punishments; there are consequences."

So, in the lead-up to my conversion to Christianity, there were a lot of religious and secular elements in my thinking. Despite my attending Catholic schools, Orthodox Christianity had at best a marginal influence on me. I had a vague belief in god, but I accepted no creed and I had no moral moorings.

Conversion to Christianity

JB: Describe your conversion to Christianity. How did you come to your present religious views and affiliation?

BD: It wasn't until two years after leaving high school in 1979 that the claims of Christianity became pressing for me. At the time, I was taking a year off from college, helping in the family business (which dealt mainly in 19th and early 20 century oil paintings).

My reasons for taking a year off from college were not happy ones for me personally. Though I had a successful high school experience academically (and academics was all that mattered to me at the time), I was unable to meet my high (and in retrospect unrealistic) expectations for college.

I left high school a year early without graduating to start at the University of Chicago, and thus lacked the seasoning, both academically and socially, that an extra year in high school would have given me. I ended up dropping a class in which I did average (right at the median), and even though my GPA ended up better than a 3.8, I felt utterly defeated.

For the next year I floundered. I had no desire or energy to pursue the academic subjects that had in the past galvanized me. Also, my New Age spirituality offered me no solace. Without meaning to sound melodramatic, I felt lost. The thought of suicide for the first time crossed my mind. Not that I was in such a grave place as imminently to act on that thought. But I understood that I was on an unhappy path and that if I wasn't able to pull away from it, suicide would for me become areal option.

It was around this time that my mother attended a Women's Aglow meeting (early 1979). I was tight with my parents, living at home at the time, and the three of us (my dad, mom, and me) were all reading books that crossed the line from self-help to New Age spirituality to outright occultism. None of our effort sat "enlightenment" had significantly improved our well-being though it occasionally led to false hopes and temporary exuberance.

So when my mom came home from that Women's Aglow meeting all buoyant about having encountered Jesus and getting saved, my reaction was that here we go again with the next thing that's going to transform our lives and make them better. And yet, the joy that my mom experienced in her conversion seemed to stick. She started plying me with Christian books and urging me to read the Bible. My response, at least initially, was cynical. And yet I read some of the material she gave me, and my dad and I occasionally went to a Christian meeting with her.

I'm not sure, how much my mom's efforts at converting my dad and me played in my own conversion. In fact, I don't recall her ever talking to me about the claims of Christianity and me in response thinking "that's right." It seemed to me I always had a wall up and resisted her urgings. And yet, I think my mom's conversion was probably pivotal in getting me to address the key question that, when I was able to answer it, was responsible for my conversion to Christianity.

Although I was never an atheist, my biggest problem religiously was seeing how God could make a meaningful connection with humanity. God was perfect, humans were in a condition of suffering. How could God really know what we were experiencing? It was in pondering this question that the Incarnation of Christ finally made sense to me. Even while attending Catholic schools, I had consciously rejected the deity of Christ. God becoming human in Jesus, and especially in experiencing the full weight of human suffering on the cross, suddenly answered my deepest question and need.

I still remember a sunny May day in 1979 walking on Sheridan Road on the north side of Chicago when that revelation hit me. I didn't become a Christian right then. It was a few days later reading alone in my room the Sermon on the Mount in Matthew's Gospel that God seemed to be asking me how long I was going to delay in accepting the truth of Christ. Then and there I got down on my knees and accepted Christ.

Within a week or so my parents and I were on a business trip to London. Sunday morning I went to

Hyde Park Speakers' Corner, knowing that I would meet some Christians there. I did. They told me about an evening service at their church and asked if there was anything I would like them to pray for. I said my dad's salvation. That night we took the Tube to the church, and my dad accepted Christ. So in about four months God had saved my immediate family.

All this happened in broadly evangelical circles. I've moved in these circles ever since.

Doubts about Unguided Evolution

JB: When did you first come to doubt that the theory of natural selection adequately explains the fact that living things appear to be designed—an appearance that even Richard Dawkins and Daniel Dennett freely admit?

BD: The funny thing—especially in light of my work on intelligent design—is that evolution played no role whatsoever in my conversion to Christianity. My dad was an evolutionist. He taught evolution at the college level. He would often joke that a few million years ago, we were swinging from trees. I accepted evolution on becoming a Christian, and I didn't see any fundamental conflict between the two.

After becoming a Christian, I started reading the creationist literature (there was no ID literature to speak of, then) and seeing the tension between Darwinism and the more conservative reading of Scripture that was customary in the evangelical circles in which I moved. But what decided me against Darwinism wasn't its unacceptability to any preferred understanding of Christianity. It was this.

We all have intuitions about what's within the reach of chance and what isn't. If I get out a fair coin and flip it three times, I might witness three heads in a row, no problem. I might even flip 10 heads in a row if given an hour or two to toss the coin. But getting 100, to say nothing of 1,000, heads in a row by chance seems completely absurd.

When I was reading about the origin of life (this was in 1980), it seemed to me utterly ridiculous that chemistry left to its own devices could pull off this feat of forming first life. Once naturalism lost its hold on me with regard to the origin of life, skepticism of Darwinism vis-à-vis the subsequent history of life followed. Indeed, without naturalism to prop up Darwinism, the evidence for this unguided form of evolution is underwhelming. Phillip Johnson showed this quite effectively in *Darwin on Trial*. Others have as well. I came to the same conclusion within a year after my conversion to Christianity.

My situation was the diametric opposite of Lee Strobel's. He lost his faith in God when he was exposed in high school to the Miller-Urey experiment, which showed that certain basic building blocks of living systems might form by chance chemistry. He mistakenly inferred that life could easily be formed without the need of any actual design or teleology. For me it was the absurdity of chance chemistry forming anything that could even remotely approach the complexity of the cell that for me undid chemical, and then Darwinian, evolution.

jgd graphic + web

Publishing Solutions ...
Book design, Prestige publications,
Annual Reports, Year Books & Magazine
production. Services include; cover & page
design, maps, charts & diagrams,
photographic art direction & illustration

Web Solutions ...
WordPress, Sitefinity & Bloomtools. Mailchimp
integration. Services include; design, project
management, construction, seo & maintenance

Video Solutions ...
Editing & Motion graphics. Social Media Ads,
Webinars with support graphics.
Supplied in Microsoft or Adobe CC

Project Quotes & Estimates ...
Ian James – 0488 069 194 (Melbourne)
Email – ian@jgd.com.au

I subsequently coauthored a book with Jonathan Wells titled *How to Be an Intellectually Fulfilled Atheist—Or Not*, keying off of Richard Dawkins's claim that Darwin made it possible to be an intellectually fulfilled atheist. The book covers the state of origin-of-life research as of 2008 and confirms that my intuitions back in the early 1980s were exactly right. Nor has subsequent research made any headway with this problem. There is no coherent account of a naturalistic origin of life. Indeed, the chemistry on which life is based, apart from any real teleology, resists the formation of the individual bio-macro molecules necessary for life, to say nothing of bringing them all together in a cell.

Reception of 'The Design Inference'

JB: We understand that what many consider to be your masterpiece so far—*The Design Inference*—is based on your Ph.D. dissertation completed two years earlier at the University of Illinois at Chicago. During the period when you were formulating the notions of specified complexity and the design inference, with whom were you in contact? Whom were you reading? What were the main intellectual influences on this seminal work?

BD: I owe specified complexity and *The Design Inference* to Richard Dawkins and, specifically, his book *The Blind Watchmaker*. I say this with some irony, but there's also some truth here. In the late 1980s, I was on my own. I had finished my Ph.D. in mathematics from the University of Chicago in 1988, gone to MIT on an NSF post doctoral fellowship, and sensed that what was fundamentally amiss in the academy was the failure to discern that God was an agent exercising real causal powers in the world. But I had no conversation partners related to this concern.

I therefore decided at MIT, against the advice of my mathematics and physics mentors, that I was going to pursue a second doctorate, this time in philosophy. Why philosophy? I knew that "philosophy of" could be attached as a prefix to just about any field of endeavor, and thus I saw philosophy as an umbrella discipline in which to explore the question of real discernible divine action, though I realized it would need to be cashed out in terms more acceptable to secular philosophers.

As I was pondering this question, I read Dawkins's *Blind Watchmaker*. I found reading it a galvanizing experience, not because the book fulfilled its promises or warranted the high praises of its fans, but because it was so interestingly wrong that it provided insight for anyone with eyes to see. At one point in that book, Dawkins writes, "Complicated things have some quality, specifiable in advance, that is highly unlikely to have been acquired by random chance alone." Right, random chance can't do it. But natural selection (or "cumulative selection" as he called it there) could? Really?

As I reflected on his argument, it became clear that natural selection would only have this capacity if it could overcome the improbabilities faced by random chance (hence his 1996 sequel, *Climbing Mount Improbable*, which nonetheless fails to round out his argument). But what if it couldn't overcome these improbabilities? Dawkins, without any real argument (the only thing he offered was his ridiculous ME THINKS IT IS LIKE A WEASEL example), simply asserted that natural selection had that power. And it would have to have that power if naturalism was correct.

But the empirical evidence simply does not support the creative power of Darwinian processes. So, the question remained: How to explain specified complexity now that the divide-and-conquer Darwinian strategy—in which natural selection would gradually build up biological complexity—could be seen to have failed?

My field in mathematics was probability, so I developed my critique of Dawkins probabilistically. Some of my critics have argued that probability is irrelevant to these discussions, but in doing so they are either uninformed or disingenuous.

Whenever biologist and ID critic Kenneth Miller, for instance, cites evidence for the power of natural selection, he appeals to some experimental set-up in which selection pressure—with high probability—brings about some biological structure/function previously lacking. But if high probability provides confirming evidence for Darwinism, why can't low probability provide dis-confirming evidence? Parity of reasoning demands that if probabilities can empirically support Darwinism, then they can also put it empirically in harm's way.

So, working alone, with my background in probability, I began to look at the probabilistic hurdles facing Darwinian natural selection and how this might provide a pointer to design. Initially, I didn't see these probabilistic arguments as making a positive case for design so much as making a negative case against naturalism. Naturalistic processes without teleology are incomplete. But it soon became clear that when probability and specification worked together, they were doing more than underscoring the incompleteness of naturalistic processes—they were pointing to a designing intelligence. I wrote a long paper outlining the key issues for the 1991 meeting of the Association of Christians in the Mathematical Sciences, which I presented at Wheaton College. It's in their proceedings volume, though not widely cited: "Reviving the Argument from Design: Detecting Design through Small Probabilities." What's missing from this paper is a full development of the concept of specified complexity and, in particular, the specification part, namely an explication of the sorts of patterns needed to reliably infer design.

After that paper and two other things I had written ("Randomness by Design" in *Nous* and "Converting Matter into Mind" in the *ASA Journal*), I came on the radar of Steve Meyer and Paul Nelson, who then connected me with the circle forming around Phil Johnson. But before that, I was feeling my way. On the one hand, it seemed clear that my work had connections with Paley-style natural theology. On the other hand, I wasn't trying to do the traditional sorts of natural-theology things, like drawing conclusions about divine attributes from nature, which seemed to me beyond the reach of my methods.

Two people whom I tried to interest in my work on design prior to joining the circle around Phil Johnson were A. E. Wilder-Smith and John Warwick Montgomery. I had corresponded with Wilder-Smith in the late 1980s. He was in Switzerland, and our *Briefwechsel* was cordial. In the summer of 1990, I went to Montgomery's summer institute on human rights in Strasbourg. Not that human rights were central to my interests, but I was single, had NSF funding, and wanted to interest Montgomery in these probabilistic arguments, thinking that they had application in the field of legal evidence, a field he had worked in. However, he had no insights to offer me.

Wilder-Smith, who resided in Switzerland not too far from some friends of mine in Freiburg, Germany, was also no help. He was a young-earth creationist and had some insightful things to say about information theory as it applied to life's origin and complexity. But when I laid out my mathematical arguments, he was dismissive—indeed, he was quite unpleasant when I called him from my friends in Freiburg. It was as though he wanted to have the final word on applying information-theoretic ideas to the origin and subsequent development of life. And yet, as a non-mathematician, he was in no position to hold that distinction, information theory being a branch of mathematics, and of probability theory in particular.

And so, disappointed by two of my biggest "intellectual heroes" (I had read their work for a decade by then), I nonetheless pressed ahead. I was convinced my approach had merit, and neither Wilder-Smith nor Montgomery offered substantive refutations. Indeed, I've always resisted deferring to people simply because of their reputations or authority.

Once I got introduced to Phil Johnson's circle, however, I did find a stimulating group of conversation partners. It was as though Providence had independently raised up a number of individuals all interested in the question of design and how it might overthrow Darwinian naturalism. Steve Meyer and Paul Nelson became my closest colleagues, with Jonathan Wells and Mike Behe close behind. And Phil was, at the time, the larger than life figure coordinating our efforts.

As for Dawkins, I've joked about dedicating one of my books to him. Of course, that would never happen, but the fact remains that Dawkins's played a crucial role in my early thoughts on intelligent design. I found his errors supremely instructive!

JB: How were your ideas initially received? Was it possible to discuss your skepticism about the ability of the natural selection mechanism to produce specified complexity freely and openly in academia at that time? If so, when did the tide begin to turn, and natural selection begin to become a sacred cow that could not be questioned without jeopardizing one's career? Was there a decisive turning point, or was it more of a gradual process?

BD: If you've read my book *The Design Inference*, and can put out of your mind my subsequent notoriety, you'll realize that the book is agnostic about chemical and biological evolution. I show, for instance, how this mode of inference applies to the origin of life, but I don't say that it leads to one conclusion or another.

Specified complexity, as a criterion for detecting design, is a method. Methods get applied to particular problem areas, but there's nothing about a method that demands, in advance, that it give a particular answer to a given state of affairs. So, by simply presenting the method, but not applying it with too much detail to controversial areas in biology, to say nothing of drawing troublesome conclusions, the book neatly sidestepped the controversy that with hindsight we see the book as engendering.

Trouble, however, was not long to be avoided. The problem is that within a month of publishing *The Design Inference*, I also published *Mere Creation*, the proceedings of a 1996 conference at Biola University on creation and design. In that book, I did put my cards on the table regarding where I saw the methods developed in *The Design Inference* as leading. So, Darwinists quickly made the connection and started going after the earlier book.

Another thing that worked against *The Design Inference* is that I was hired shortly after its publication to found and direct Baylor's Michael Polanyi Center (1999). This gave me and intelligent design national prominence, to the consternation of Darwinists in- and outside of Baylor, and thus incentivized them to undermine my work, and that book in particular. Here was a research center dedicated to intelligent design at a major university—it didn't take a genius to see in this a slippery slope!

When the Polanyi Center was dissolved a year later (more about this below), many who had their finger to the wind and wondered whether to back intelligent design, backed down. I stayed on at Baylor to complete my contract, but was *persona non grata* my entire time there.

In retrospect, I should have gotten away from Baylor as quickly as possible—it was deeply unhealthy to me personally and to my family to stay in so hostile a place. But I was much more the fighter at the time and I wanted vindication, which I never got there and which I was foolish to think I could get there. My biggest regret about that time is not the loss to my career but the distress to my family.

One particularly telling aspect of my time at Baylor is that campus publications, which would otherwise make a point of touting the accomplishments of faculty, pretended I didn't exist. Baylor was at the time especially interested in work promoting a rapprochement between learning and faith. In both 2000 and 2005 I received *Christianity Today*'s book award for the category "Christianity and Culture" (for my books *Intelligent Design* and *The Design Revolution* respectively),books clearly at the intersection of faith and learning. Neither award was ever mentioned in any campus publication, to say nothing of any other books, articles, or media appearances I had during my time at Baylor.

In any case, in 1999, I could still get a job in the mainstream academy on the basis of my work in *The Design Inference*. By the fall of 2000, my academic career was toast.

Fellow of Discovery Institute

JB: You have been a Fellow with the Discovery Institute (DI) in Seattle since 1996. They have played an important role in disseminating your ideas, and ID more generally, to the general public. Both you and they are also frequently targets of attack by the academic establishment and the political left. Can you tell us a little bit about the DI, and about your role there?

BD: I was a fellow of Discovery Institute's Center for Science and Culture (the ID arm of Discovery) from 1996 to 2016. At the end of that time, I largely retired from intelligent design and resigned my fellowship. I continue to have connections with Discovery Institute, but my life and work are these days focused elsewhere.

The Discovery Institute's founding dates back to the early 1990s. It was started as a high-tech public-policy think tank. George Gilder was one of its early visionaries. In the mid-1990s, Steve Meyer came on their radar, and the then director of Discovery, Bruce Chapman, decided to establish a program headed by Meyer to promote intelligent design. Think of Discovery Institute as an incubator for various initiatives. The ID initiative quickly became Discovery Institute's main initiative and the one for which it is best known.

When Meyer became the director of the newly founded Center for the Renewal of Science and Culture (subsequently simplified to the Center for Science and Culture), he included me among its initial, fully funded fellows. This was a godsend. I was newly married, and the job market was tough in philosophy at the time. Coming on board with Discovery allowed me to pursue research in ID full-time. It made a huge difference to my subsequent research.

I stayed on as a full-time Discovery fellow until Baylor hired me in early 2000. But in the intervening time, Discovery provided support, both tangible and intangible. As it is, I left my faculty position at Southwestern Seminary in 2012 and returned as a full-time fellow of Discovery for the next two years. This allowed me to complete the third volume in my ID trilogy, *Being as Communion: A Metaphysics of Information* (published with Ashgate in 2014—the other two volumes in the trilogy being *The Design Inference* and *No Free Lunch*). Beginning in 2015 I turned my attention principally to education.

Throughout the years, my role with Discovery has been to develop intelligent design's theoretical underpinnings, both with statistical and logical analyses of design-inferential reasoning and with information-theoretic analyses of evolutionary searches. This work has meshed with work of other Discovery fellows.

Discovery Institute has had a hand in most of the ID movement's successes. Perhaps the same can be said for the movement's failures. In any case, the ID movements overarching goal, namely, ID's victory over Darwinian naturalism as the reigning paradigm in biology, is far from being a done deal.

Certainly, Discovery Institute has provided ID researchers with support and even protection. For some of us, this proved crucial in enabling us to stay engaged in the debate over evolution and design. In my own case, when Baylor tried to terminate my appointment in 2000, Discovery Institute paid my attorney's fees, after which I had a secure position at Baylor for the duration of my 5-year contract (even if I was *persona non grata* with a closet for an office, that closet was secure).

But writing now with over 20 years' hindsight, I also

think that Discovery Institute has in ways undercut its effectiveness in promoting intelligent design. If I had to put my finger on the main problem here, it's the conflation of politics with science. That such a conflation would happen is understandable: for a think tank to pull in funding, especially about so controversial a view as ID, it's natural that the people funding ID would do so not for purely scientific purposes, but because of the mileage they hoped to get out of it politically (and here I'm using "politics" very generally to include everything from ordinary politics to law to culture, and even to religion).

The infamous "Wedge Strategy," unveiled by Discovery in 1998, is emblematic of this problem of conflating politics and science. On the one hand, Discovery was committed to funding researchers like me to develop ID's scientific and intellectual credentials. But at the same time it was also promoting a Wedge Strategy in which ID would be used to undermine the naturalistic worldview inherent in so much of American culture, especially in the media, courts, and academy.

To promote ID as science would be to treat it as an essential good, as something to be pursued simply because it provided true insights into the natural world, and thus because such scientific truths are valuable in their own right. But to promote ID as politics would be to treat it as an instrumental good, as something to be pursued because of non-scientific benefits to be reaped. Discovery was not alone in using ID as an instrumental good. My seminary appointments, in which I was hired to promote ID as a way of shoring up traditional understandings of creation, were in this same vein. Obviously, I'm as guilty here as anyone, complicit in treating ID as both an essential and an instrumental good.

It's no accident that Discovery's center for promoting ID, which is also where the Wedge Strategy originated, was called The Center for Science and Culture. In retrospect, I think the ID movement would be further along as a scientific and intellectual project if Discovery could have focused purely on promoting ID as science and left politics in all its guises aside from this debate. I don't know if this would have been possible from a fund-raising perspective (who would have funded it in that case?).

But if I had to do it all again, I would have set aside the political dimension of intelligent design, perhaps even forgoing the books I wrote on the theological and philosophical implications of ID until the science was firmly in place. This, it seems, would also have helped mitigate the strident rhetoric so often associated with the ID community, in which I certainly engaged (especially between 2005 and 2010 on my blog UncommonDescent.com), and which has been evident in Discovery publications (such as its EvolutionNews.org blog).

But hypotheticals about what might have been don't change anything. And the fact is that ID, like its Darwinian competitor, has deep worldview connections that many other scientific theories lack. So perhaps there was no clean way to develop ID scientifically without also developing its cultural and political implications.

Intelligent Design—Science or Pseudoscience?

JB: You have stated that "design theorists oppose Darwinian theory on strictly scientific grounds." But then why is the ID movement so heavily populated with religious believers? Could we not expect more of the scientific community to support ID if your statement were true? Why do the majority of the world's leading scientific bodies oppose ID and claim that it does not qualify as science?

BD: The quote needs context. I've also written that intelligent design, besides being a scientific program, has a theological dimension, in trying to understand divine action, and a cultural dimension, in trying to overturn naturalism. So intelligent design is a number of things. But at its core, it is a scientific program. Indeed, unless there is good science to back it up, all the cultural and theological superstructures that people build on it will be in vain.

As for why religious believers tend to be associated with design, I could turn the question around. If Darwinian evolution is strictly scientific, then why is that field so heavily populated with atheists? In one survey of around 150 prominent evolutionary biologists, only two were religious believers (as I recall, Will Provine was behind this survey). I see a scientific core to both intelligent design and Darwinian evolution. And I see no merit in questioning their scientific status by the company they keep. The character of the proposals that both approaches make is what really ought to count.

But why, then, have so many scientific bodies turned against ID? I recall speaking at a symposium at Grove City College back in 2007, and University of Wisconsin historian of science Ron Numbers mentioning that over 100 professional scientific societies had issued formal denunciations of intelligent design. Since that time I don't recall any scientific body coming out in favor of intelligent design or even taking a neutral stance with respect to it.

Even so, I've been unimpressed with these denunciations. In every case, they have seemed to me politically motivated, attempting to ensure that the professional society doesn't lose face should some of its wayward members be perceived as sympathizing with ID. I recall the AAAS denunciation of ID. I was a member at the time, though I let my membership lapse subsequently because of that denunciation. When colleagues of mine inquired into who was behind the AAAS denunciation and what materials they had read that convinced them to issue it, it became clear that key materials were unread and the denouncers were woefully ignorant, not understand what they were denouncing.

As for more scientists coming on board with ID if it were legitimate, I think this question confuses legitimacy with incentives. There are no incentives for coming on board with ID other than the personal satisfaction of contemplating interesting ideas and true insights about certain salient patterns in nature. And that's hardly enough for many professionals, who seem all too willing to sacrifice their lives and principles to advance their careers. There is no federal funding for ID research. If it's known that you accept intelligent design and you're in the mainstream academy, you can expect your career to be derailed. Support ID and expect pain.

On the other hand, if you denounce intelligent design, you score points. Think of Judge Jones in the *Dover v. Kitzmiller* case. After ruling against ID in 2005, he was voted one of 2005's ten most sexy geeks by *Wired* magazine. *Time* magazine voted him one of the 100 most important thinkers of 2005. And last I heard, he had been awarded four honorary doctorates (I've confirmed two of them). Jones's claim to fame prior to *Dover* was not expertise in the theoretical underpinnings of evolutionary biology, but rather heading the Pennsylvania Liquor Commission.

I could recount cases of unimpressive academics who have done very well for themselves (tenure, named professorships, etc.) by denouncing ID. And I can recount cases of very bright individuals whose careers have been derailed for supporting, or even showing sympathy toward, ID. The documentary *Expelled* demonstrates this last point.

Ben Stein's Documentary on ID

JB: In bringing up *Expelled*, you beat me to the punch. You were prominently featured in a documentary favorable to intelligent design, narrated by Ben Stein and titled *Expelled: No Intelligence Allowed*. What can you tell us about that documentary? Did it help or hurt the ID movement?

BD: The documentary came out in the spring of 2008 and most of the footage was taken the year earlier. I was there forecalled in as a background or resource person—in the few spots I have in the movie, that's what I do, i.e., provide background information. I could well have been one of the "expelled," but my story of being "expelled" at Baylor goes back to 2000 and the producers were looking for more recent narratives.

I would give the documentary a B, certainly not an A. It effectively underscores the opposition that proponents of intelligent design face in the academy. Some of the individual cases recounted pack a nice punch. And the "exit interview" by Richard Dawkins with Ben Stein is classic. Stein gets Dawkins to admit that ID might be legitimate, so long as the designer is not God but a space alien who evolved by Darwinian means. When I used to give public lectures on ID, I almost always showed that clip. Indeed, Dawkins gives away the store in those few minutes.

But the documentary had some weaknesses. The seven or so minutes devoted to the Nazis and their assimilation of Darwinian theory and its basis in the holocaust was misplaced. Not that there isn't a connection, but bringing up the Nazis invariably causes the temperature to rise and the train of an argument to be lost. Far better would have been to use those seven minutes to recount the record of accomplishment of intelligent design. This, to me, was the biggest weakness of the movie. So what if ID is marginalized and its proponents vilified? But what has it accomplished to show that it doesn't deserve that treatment? This needed to be spelled out, and the film didn't do that.

Also, the producers mismanaged their funds. *Expelled* was to lead to a national discussion, with an active website from which people could learn more about ID. The weekend that the documentary opened in theaters, however, the website went dormant—the producers had run out of funds. The film could have done much better at the box office with some more careful editing and refocusing of the material. And its impact, even as it is, would have been far greater if the intended support structures, such as the website, had been fully functioning.

One bit of hype leading up to the release of Expelled was a Jib Jab-style video titled "Richard Dawkins: Beware the Believers".

The video was light and clever, and even put fear in some evolutionists, who expressed the worry that *Expelled* might signal a major step forward in ID's public relations and cultural engagement. Unfortunately, as noted, the people behind *Expelled* ran out of money opening weekend, and any internet help to promote *Expelled* there after largely vanished.

Even so, with the documentary out on DVD and through streaming, I continue to hear from people who've seen me in it (some from my distant past). On balance, I think it's had a positive impact in alerting people to the controversy over intelligent design.

The Michael Polanyi Center

JB: In 2000, after organizing and hosting a very

successful and visible international conference (whose proceedings, coedited by you and Bruce Gordon, are now published as *The Nature of Nature* [ISI, 2011]), you were first demoted, then essentially fired, by Baylor University, in Waco, Texas. Can you explain how this came about? What were the ramifications of Baylor throwing you under the bus for you personally? What do you think the long-term ramifications of this incident have been for our intellectual culture as a whole?

BD: Briefly, Baylor hired me to start an intelligent design think-tank, the Michael Polanyi Center, we put on a tremendously successful conference, and three days after the conference the faculty senate voted 27–2 to shut the center down. Not immediately, but a few months later, the Baylor administration acceded to the faculty senate's wishes.

When I protested the center's dissolution, I was fired as director from a center that had already ceased to exist. This, at Baylor—an ostensibly Christian institution. But in fact, the science faculty at Baylor were probably more Darwinian than their secular counterparts, having to prove that they were as "reliable" in their science as those in the mainstream secular academy.

The whole story is available online, arranged chronologically in a series of news articles: "The Rise and Fall of Baylor University's Michael Polanyi Center." If I had it to do again, I would never have gone to Baylor. But the past is past. It's all there. It made national news. And Baylor got a black eye for its failure to respect freedom of thought and expression.

But massive institutions like Baylor can handle a bit of battering. Private individuals who get chewed up by them are less fortunate.

The bottom line is that ID remains without the sort of institutional support that could accelerate its research and acceptance. I give the Darwinists credit here for their implacable opposition to ID. The Polanyi Center was the first and remains the last ID center at any college or university. It's a sad commentary, not just on higher education, but on Christian higher education specifically.

[The previous paragraph was part of the 2016 interview. In 2019, Biola University hired molecular biologist Douglas Axe, a prominent ID proponent, giving him also an endowed professorship. Provided that he has funding and can openly pursue ID research in collaboration with fellow faculty, postdocs, and students at Biola, then it would be fair to say that Biola has at long last superseded Baylor's erstwhile Polanyi Center.]

One of the main lessons I've drawn from my experience at Baylor is that most of the academic world, Christian included, is not so much concerned with truth as with fitting in and looking good. Perhaps I should have known that from the start. After the Polanyi Center closed, so too did much of the sympathy toward and curiosity about ID. In many people's minds, ID was no longer a winner, and people like to be associated with a winner. We saw the same phenomenon a few years later with the *Dover* trial.

But history teaches that truth has little to do with winning and losing. Christ—the one who calls himself "the way, the truth, and the light"— is hardly a picture of victory on the Cross. So, I never lose heart.

For me personally, the Baylor episode has been better in the aftermath than in its unfolding at the time. Lots of people rallied to me. And I gained many valuable conversation partners. I had enough visibility and support so that I could land on my feet. But it could easily have turned out worse.

As for the ramifications of this incident for our culture as a whole, I don't want to read too much into this. I don't think it should be read as a decisive battle that changes the course of a war. Rather, I would see it as emblematic of the corruption that already existed in the academy. This incident merely underscored the degree to which secular ideology was and remains entrenched in the academy.

JB: When the Baylor Faculty Senate voted just a few days after the Nature of Nature conference to request that the Baylor Administration dissolve the Center, the Administration appointed an External Review Committee whose report, while commending Baylor's scientific community, also endorsed the work of the Center by suggesting that it expand its vision and change its name to reflect that broader scope. Your press release in response hailed the Committee's report as a victory not only for academic freedom, but also for intelligent design "as a legitimate form of academic inquiry." The final two sentences of your press release, however, understandably created an uproar: "Dogmatic opponents of design who demanded the Center be shut down have met their Waterloo. Baylor University is to be commended for remaining strong in the face of intolerant assaults on freedom of thought and expression." Looking back on the firestorm that ensued from that press release, do you think you might have been hasty and do you regret the wording? Could the Polanyi Center have survived if you had been more "temperate" in your choice of words? What's the real story here?

BD: Many have interpreted my press release and the now infamous "Waterloo" comment (it was widely reported in the press at the time and to this day can be found using the search engines) as an intemperate challenge by a feisty academic who should have known when to shut up. Here is the real story. In May of 2000, before the review committee was installed, I was invited to speak on Capitol Hill before members of Congress. This was a bipartisan briefing—not a hearing—so there was no policy or law to be enacted on the basis of my remarks.

The Baylor administration, despite installing me as director of the Polanyi Center with duties to raise monies for the center, forbade me from attending this conference. I decided to accede to their wishes (despite the clear violation of my academic freedom), but when a press release mistakenly appeared saying that I would be at the meeting on Capitol Hill after all, the Baylor campus was in an uproar and the Baylor administration drafted a letter which they wanted me to sign, addressed to the Baylor community and assuring them that I was not going to the Capitol Hill briefing because that would politicize intelligent design, something I could not do as director of the Polanyi Center.

I told the administration that I did not attend the briefing out of courtesy to them because of all the pressure they were under on account of the Polanyi Center, but that I would not sign the letter because I saw it as well within my prescribed duties to attend such meetings and that in the future I would do so. They reacted very negatively to this. In fact, they wanted to settle with me right then and there and show me to the door. I had to get a lawyer and after two months of negotiations they offered me a pittance to buy me out of a five and a half year contract. I told them to forget it and that I would be moving to Waco, where Baylor is located (I was living at the time in the Dallas area). All this happened summer of 2000.

When the review committee finally met in September of 2000, it was a star chamber. I was grilled. All my works were scrutinized. I had no recourse to anyone on or outside campus. Unlike tenure review decisions, all the findings of the committee would be made public. Biologist John Moore, one of the persons on the committee, was interviewed in the local paper the day before the committee met with me and told the reporter that I was clever but that my work was not scientific but political. So the deck was stacked against me.

When the committee issued its report a month later, they made four recommendations: (1) drop the name of the Polanyi Center; (2) absorb whatever entity it might become into Baylor's Institute for Faith and Learning (in which I had no administrative authority); (3) change the emphasis of whatever this center might become from the scientific investigation of intelligent design to that fuzzy catch-all category known as "science and religion"; and (4) institute an advisory board to determine what should be done on the Baylor campus with regard to science and religion issues. In short, there was no more Polanyi Center.

The Baylor administration immediately signed off on these recommendations. I was to have been given two days notice about the review committee's recommendations and the Baylor administration's decision whether to adopt them. Instead, I learned of the recommendations Monday late afternoon. By Tuesday morning the review committee's report was broadcast all over the Internet along with the Baylor administration's full endorsement. By Tuesday afternoon the press was after me for comment. I therefore decided to issue the press release to which you referred. The one bright spot in the peer review committee report was that they said my work had legitimacy (albeit as a contribution to the relation between science and religion). I therefore highlighted this concession to the legitimacy of my work in the press release.

On the other hand, my whole purpose for coming to Baylor had been thwarted—I did not come to Baylor to uncover ID's religious implications but to develop ID as a scientific research program. My "Waterloo" comment was meant to underscore the irony, indeed the ridiculousness, of these entire proceedings. The Baylor faculty eager to shut down the Polanyi Center were humorless. Rather than seeing the irony and understanding that they had been completely victorious in crushing the Polanyi Center, they agitated still further, thereby **compounding the irony. Thus the Baylor president, after shutting down the**

Polanyi Center, went further and fired me from a center that no longer existed. I may still have that letter.

Seminary Teaching

JB: After leaving Baylor in 2005, you taught full-time at Southern Seminary in Louisville and Southwestern Seminary in Ft. Worth. What was it like teaching at these Southern Baptist institutions? Did you enjoy it? When you were working on your doctorates in mathematics and philosophy, would you have imagined that you might be teaching full-time at conservative Baptist theological seminaries?

BD: These institutions gave me the opportunity to teach when just about no one else would hire me. They helped me to keep the wolf away from the door, and for that I'm grateful. But the experience did not end well for me. I had been too conservative for Baylor. I ended up being too liberal for the conservative Southern Baptists, for whom young-earth creationism increasingly became a litmus test of orthodoxy. More on that shortly.

How did I end up with conservative Southern Baptists? One needs to understand that intelligent design is not just anathema to atheistic evolutionists like Richard Dawkins; it is doubly anathema to theistic evolutionists, who see it as both bad science and bad theology.

This may sound crazy to outsiders, who see Christianity as historically teaching special creation and design.

But for theistic evolutionists, who have made their accommodation with Darwin, to question evolution is to open a can of worms that, in their minds, should have been closed long ago. So, when Baylor refused to renew my contract in 2005, I had very few options. Most of the CCCU schools (Council for Christian Colleges and Universities) would never hire me, or any of my colleagues known to be publicly identified with ID. That includes Wheaton, Calvin College, Westmont, Seattle Pacific, Messiah, etc., etc.

Initially, I enjoyed teaching at Southern Baptist theological seminaries. I especially liked engaging young people with fire in the belly, energy, and passion to attempt great things. If initially I had any reservations about teaching full-time at a theological institution, it's that my colleagues were focused on philosophical and theological issues.

My own interests were always broader. Even as I was teaching at theological seminaries, I saw my main work as making intelligent design into a fruitful and credible scientific research program. I'm a scientist at heart. Indeed, through most of my time as a theology professor, I was also a research scientist with Baylor engineer Bob Marks's ID research group, the Evolutionary Informatics Lab.

The seminaries at which I worked gave me space to pursue my ID research (notably by giving me a reduced course load). But my focus on ID meant that much of my work, even as a full-time seminary professor, had to be conducted outside that community.

Rewind the tape and ask me if I thought I'd be teaching

at a theological seminary, and I would have said no. But with a philosophy PhD and an MDiv, I was qualified to teach at seminary, and necessity required that I do so. I enjoyed the teaching, at least initially. Seminary politics, the savage lurch of Southern Baptist theological education into fundamentalism during my time there, and the decimation of the philosophy department at Southwestern Seminary while I was a faculty member all conspired to hasten my exit from seminary teaching.

The Evolutionary Informatics Lab

JB: You wear many hats. We've just discussed your affiliation with Discovery Institute and the theological world. Beating us to the punch again, you are also a senior research scientist with the Evolutionary Informatics Lab, which was formerly at Baylor. Tell us about your association with that lab? It appears that you have been publishing extensively in the peer-reviewed engineering and mathematical literature on active information. How is that work related to intelligent design?

How much attention has it been getting?

BD: Since 2006, my main work on intelligent design has been in collaboration with Robert Marks, a senior and high-profile engineer on the faculty at Baylor. Even though I was teaching in Ft. Worth at Southwestern Seminary after leaving Baylor, I continued to live in the Waco area, which is the home of Baylor. So, Bob and I would continue to meet regularly to discuss our research until 2012, when I left seminary teaching and moved to Iowa (for family reasons—we have severely autistic son and needed the support of my wife's family, which is from Iowa). Bob was also able to bring in some talented graduate students to help with this research. All these efforts were organized under a lab that Bob founded: The Evolutionary Informatics Lab.

The lab used to be one of Bob's several labs at Baylor, but when he was interviewed back in 2007 by Casey Luskin for a Discovery Institute podcast, it became public knowledge that the lab's research was related to ID. That was a no-no as far as then Baylor president John Lilley was concerned. In consequence, Bob was told by his dean (at Lilley's instance) to dissociate the lab from Baylor by removing that work from his space on the Baylor server. When he refused, the Baylor administration did it for him. That unhappy episode is featured in *Expelled*.

The term "evolutionary informatics" was chosen deliberately and was meant to signify that evolution, conceived as a search, requires information to be successful as in locating a target. This need for information can be demonstrated mathematically in the modeling of evolutionary processes. So, the question then becomes: Where does the information that enables evolutionary searches to be successful come from in the first place? Bob and I show that Darwinian processes at best shuffle around existing information, but can't create the information needed for successful evolutionary searches from scratch.

We've shown this in various theoretical articles, published in such places as *Journal of Advanced Computation al Intelligence* and *Intelligent Informatics*.

And we've done it in various application articles, where we look at concrete computational scenarios proposed by evolutionists (such as Avida or Tierra) and demonstrate where the information needed for them to be successful is inserted (rather than generated from scratch). This work has also been published and presented in standard engineering venues, such as IEEE [Institute of Electrical and Electronics Engineers—ed.] journals and conferences. All told, we have over twenty articles, many peer-reviewed and others conference presentations, related to conservation of information.

These results on evolutionary informatics provide the most powerful theoretical challenge by intelligent design against Darwinian evolution to date. As for the attention this work has garnered, there has been some, but Darwinists are largely ignoring it. I'm inclined to think (and with some justification) that this is because our methods leave Darwinists no loopholes. We're not saying that evolution doesn't happen. And we're not saying the Darwinian mechanism is ineffective. We're saying that even if evolution happens and happens by Darwinian means, it requires an information source beyond the reach of any unguided evolutionary mechanisms.

Here's an irony. Jeff Shallit, a former professor of mine in computational number theory at the University of Chicago, spent the better part of one sabbatical going after my 2002 book *No Free Lunch: Why Specified Complexity Cannot be Purchased without Intelligence*. To his credit, he found a few errors (nothing major), such as a probability calculation that was numerically wrong, but whose right answer was still within the universal probability bound that I had established, thus not changing the validity of my argument.

During his sabbatical, Shallit had telephoned me out of the blue and urged me to write up more detailed mathematical accounts of my ideas in *No Free Lunch*, submitting them for publication to technical journals.

This I did in my work with Bob Marks through the Evolutionary Informatics Lab. Yet, when I presented Shallit with some of this newer work on evolutionary informatics, he emailed me back saying he wasn't even going to look at it because I hadn't in his view adequately responded to his prior critiques. My Wikipedia bio, which cites Shallit's criticisms of me, last I looked, also says nothing about my actual publications on evolutionary informatics or the significance of that work, merely mentioning my association with the lab and its expulsion from Baylor. Indeed, I've tried to get my Wikipedia bio corrected on a number of points, but always in vain. Wikipedia is fine for lots of things, but on controversial topics with biased editors, it can be quite bad.

Although it would seem that this work on evolutionary informatics is getting ignored, I wonder whether in fact it is being taken seriously, only left unmentioned publicly lest it receive legitimacy simply by being on the mouths of our critics. I've seen this before. Robert Pennock, for instance, in a *Nature* article purporting to show how, in the Avida computer simulation, evolutionary processes can build complex structures and functions, omits any reference to Michael Behe and his work on intelligent design.

And yet, in my 2004 Cambridge University Press anthology, coedited with Michael Ruse and entitled *Debating Design: From Darwin to DNA*, Pennock, who has an article there, gloats that this work refutes Behe. Why didn't he make that point in the *Nature* article? Most likely because citing Behe there would have given Behe another mention in the science citation index and thus further legitimized his efforts to advance intelligent design. I've seen the same thing with my own work, which is clearly in the background of some scientific discussions, but doesn't get cited lest it be legitimized.

Another thing that makes me think that this work is having an impact is that after research at the Evolutionary Informatics Lab started gaining momentum (the publications page there now has quite an impressive collection of titles), Michigan State University, home of Pennock's Digital Evolution Lab, received a huge $25 million NSF grant in 2010 for BEACON (Bio-computational Evolution in Action CONsortium). I suspect that at least part of the rationale for the NSF giving our tax dollars to fund this boon doggle is the threat to Darwinian evolution posed by the Evolutionary Informatics Lab.

For a full discussion of evolutionary informatics in a single place, see my 2017 book with Bob Marks and Winston Ewert titled *Introduction to Evolutionary Informatics* (published by World Scientific).

Disillusion with Fundamentalism

JB: In a debate with Christopher Hitchens in 2010, you cite Boethius in saying that goodness is a problem for the atheist in the same way that evil is a problem for the theist. We would like to hear more about both sides of this interesting observation. First, the problem of evil, which is a main topic of your book *The End of Christianity: Finding a Good God in an Evil World* (B&H Academic, 2009). For the sake of our readers: The "problem of evil" is the apparent incompatibility of evil with the omnipotence and goodness of God. In a nutshell, could you tell us about your personal take on this perennial problem?

BD: My basic line on the problem of evil is the very traditional Christian view that God allows evil temporarily because of the greater good that ultimately results from having allowed it. My entire prepared remarks in the debate with Hitchens are available online. I encourage readers of this interview to look at it.

What I was dealing with in *The End of Christianity* is a more narrow problem, namely, how to account for evil within a Christian framework given a reading of Genesis that allows the earth and universe to be billions, rather than merely thousands, of years old. I'm an old-earth creationist, so I accept that the earth and universe are billions of years old. Young-earth creationism, which is the more traditional view, holds that the earth is only thousands of years old.

The reason this divergence between young-earth and

old-earth creationists is relevant to the problem of evil is that Christians have traditionally believed that both moral and natural evil are a consequence of the fall of humanity. But natural evil, such as animals killing and parasitizing each other, would predate the arrival of humans on the scene if the earth is old and animal life preceded them. So, how could their suffering be a consequence of human sin and the Fall? My solution is to argue that the Fall had retroactive effects in history (much as the salvation of Christ on the Cross acts not only forward in time to save people now, but also backward in time to save the Old Testament saints).

The book is a piece of speculative theology, and I'm not convinced of all of its details. It's been interesting, however, to see the reaction in some Christian circles, especially the fundamentalist ones. Ken Ham went ballistic over it, going around the country denouncing me as a heretic, and encouraging people to write to my theological employers to see to it that I get fired for the views I take in it.

At one point in the book, I examine what evolution would look like within the framework I lay out. Now, I'm not an evolutionist. I don't hold to universal common ancestry. I believe in a real Adam and Eve (i.e., an original human pair) specially created by God apart from primate ancestors. Friends used to joke that my conservativism, both politically and theologically, put me to the right of Attila the Hun. And yet, for merely running the logic of how a retroactive view of the Fall would look from the vantage of Darwinian theory (which I don't accept), I received email after email calling me a compromiser and someone who has sold out the faith (the emails are really quite remarkable).

There's a mentality I see prevalent in conservative Christian circles that one can never be quite conservative enough. This got me thinking about fundamentalism and the bane it is. It's one thing to hold views passionately. It's another to hold one particular view so dogmatically that all others may not even be discussed, or their logical consequences considered. This worries me about the future of evangelicalism.

When I first began following the conservative resurgence among Southern Baptists in the 1990s, I embraced it. As it is, I did my theological education at Princeton Seminary, which was representative of the theological liberalism that to my mind had sold out the faith. The pattern that always seemed to repeat itself was that Christian institutions and denominations that had started out faithful to the Gospel eventually veered away and denied their original faith.

With the Southern Baptists, that dismal trend finally seemed to be reversed. Some of the Baptist seminaries were by the late '80s and early '90s as liberal as my Princeton Seminary. And yet, the Southern Baptist Convention reversed course and took back their seminaries, attempting to reestablish Christian orthodoxy. This was refreshing at the time.

But Christian orthodoxy is one thing. A "canst thou be more conservative than I?" mentality is another. And this is the mentality that I saw emerging, in real time, after the conservative Southern Baptists took back their seminaries.

What's behind this hyper-conservative/fundamentalist mentality is a sense of beleaguerment by the wider culture and a desire for simple, neat, pat solutions. Life is messy and the Bible is not a book of systematic theology, but to the fundamentalist mind, this is unacceptable. My book *The End of Christianity* has, more than any of my other books (and I've done over 20), been an eye-opener to me personally in the reaction it elicited. The reaction of Darwinists and theistic evolutionists to my work, though harsh, is predictable. The reaction of fundamentalists was to me surprising, though in hindsight I should have expected it.

Why was it surprising to me? I suppose because during my time at Princeton and Baylor, I myself was always characterized as a fundamentalist. "Fundamentalist" is a term of abuse (Al Plantinga has described it as "a term of abuse or disapprobation, rather like 'son of a bitch', more exactly 'son ova bitch'"). But I intend fundamentalism here in a particular sense.

Fundamentalism, as I'm using it, is not concerned with any doctrinal position, however conservative or traditional. What's at stake is a harsh, wooden-headed attitude that not only insists on one's rightness, but refuses to listen to, learn from, or understand other Christians, to say nothing of outsiders to the faith. Fundamentalism in this sense is a brain-dead, soul-stifling attitude. I see it as a huge danger for evangelicals.

For a concrete example of fundamentalism at its worst, consider how hyper-conservatives, pushing a jaundiced view of biblical inerrancy, have treated my good friend, colleague, and collaborator Mike Licona (we coedited a book titled *Evidence for God: 50 Arguments for Faith from the Bible, History, Philosophy, and Science*). Even though he holds to the entirely traditional view that Jesus resurrected bodily from the dead, and even though he is by any accounts conservative in his understanding of the New Testament's historical reliability, he isn't quite conservative enough for the hyper-conservatives.

Why? Because he questions whether the account in Matthew 27 of Old Testament saints bursting their tombs and walking around Jerusalem might best be taken allegorically. In consequence, Licona has been ostracized by much of the seminary world in which I used to teach and lecture.

I've digressed. Let me return to your question on the "problem of good." This problem poses an obvious and devastating refutation of the materialist position the moment one reflects on it. Whence the indignation of the New Atheists against the injustices and evils in the world, if the world is without real value, if it is, as Richard Dawkins puts it, a place of "pitiless indifference"? What is so exercising these New Atheists, what is so passionately arousing their outrage? Is it not that some real good has been violated? Yet in the absence of any real good, what is there to get excited about? In that case, good and bad are simply labels that we apply based on our evolutionary conditioning, labels that could be interchanged given different evolutionary conditioning.

The irony that the New Atheists presuppose some

conception of real good gets compounded when they need to explain holocaust rescuers or someone like Mother Teresa. I purposely ended my formal remarks in the debate with Christopher Hitchens by citing Mother Teresa. I knew this would be like waving a red flag in front of a bull. Hitchens had done a documentary and then written a book claiming she was a fraud. True to form, Hitchens went on a rant against her once I brought her up, which did not help him in the debate. Hitchens is not the only atheist who needed to explain away Mother Teresa's acts of charity. E. O. Wilson has done the same. In a world so filled with evil, why go after Mother Teresa? Because, despite her faults, if her goodness is left unchallenged, it challenges a materialistic worldview that at bottom has no substantive values. It's fine, on such a view, for values to be explained as culturally or evolutionarily conditioned. But real goodness that transcends such relativism is unacceptable.

JB: Your digression concerning the fundamentalist reaction to your book *The End of Christianity* is in fact no digression at all. We want to ask you about a strange episode involving that book that occurred in 2010 shortly after its publication, while you were still teaching at Southwestern Baptist Theological Seminary. Tom Nettles, a professor at The Southern Baptist Theological Seminary, where you had previously taught, wrote a scathing review of *The End of Christianity*. In response, the president of your seminary, Paige Patterson, as well as the dean issued a white paper defending you and your work in this book, sort of. In that white paper you had a four-paragraph statement, whose main purpose seems to be to assure readers of your orthodoxy. It all feels very carefully choreographed. What was up with that?

BD: The white paper you describe and the events surrounding it are, probably more than anything, the reason I'm no longer teaching at theological seminaries. Indeed, this entire incident left so bad a taste in my mouth that I resolved to leave teaching, leave the academy, and get into a business for myself, in which my income would not depend on political correctness or, for that matter, theological correctness.

Sometimes I marvel at my own naiveté. I wrote *The End of Christianity* thinking that it might be a way to move young-earth creationists from their position that the earth and universe are only a few thousand years old by addressing the first objection that they invariably throw at an old-earth position, namely, the problem of natural evil before the Fall. I thought that by proposing my retroactive view of the Fall, that I was addressing their concern and thus that I might see some positive movement toward my old-earth position.

I couldn't have been more wrong. As a professional therapist once put it to me, the presenting problem is never the real problem. I quickly found out that the young-earth theologians I was dealing with were far less concerned about how the Fall could be squared with an old earth than with simply preserving the most obvious interpretation of Genesis 1–3, namely, that the earth and universe are just a few thousand years old. Again, we're talking the fundamentalist impulse to simple, neat, pat answers. Now I'll readily grant that the appeal to complexity can be a way of evading the truth. But so can the appeal to simplicity, and fundamentalism loves to keep things simple.

In any case, after the review of Tom Nettles appeared, I sensed a shift against me at Southwestern Seminary where I was teaching. Previously I had been a golden boy, with my visage even being used to advertise the seminary in publications such as *World Magazine*. Now, however, fellow faculty showed a solicitude for me that I had not seen before, as though I might be facing the gallows.

Perhaps I was. I was to meet in the president's office, and those present would include the president, the provost, the dean of theology, and one of the senior professors. I knew that I was not up for the Nobel Prize or any honor that might warrant a meeting with such an estimable assembly. And so, I drew the obvious and correct conclusion that I was in a heap of trouble.

Fortunately, I was at the time a visible figure in the evangelical world. I had been cashiered by Baylor, and this was widely reported in the evangelical press, to the detriment of Baylor. Presumably, the Southwestern administration would be reluctant to make a similar example of me. One of my friends on the Southwestern faculty telegraphed me where the problem lay: my supposedly unorthodox views on Noah's flood—I kid you not.

Strictly speaking, my project in *The End of Christianity* centered on the interpretation of Genesis 1–3. But at the very end of the book, I raised some questions about Noah's flood in light of an old earth (Noah appears in Genesis 6–9). I never thought the matter through very closely, but it seemed to me if one had latitude in interpreting Genesis 1–3, then one could have some latitude here. I suggested as much in *The End of Christianity*.

At the meeting with president, provost, dean, and senior professor, the president made it clear to me from the start that my job was on the line. "Job on the line" in this context does not mean finishing out the academic year and giving me a chance to find another academic job. My questioning the universality of Noah's flood meant I was a heretic—unsuitable for teaching at Southern Baptist seminaries because a danger to impressionable young minds. And thus I'd need to be clearing my desk immediately—unless my theological soundness could be quickly be reestablished.

With a severely autistic son, debts, and a family still upset about my experience at Baylor, I wasn't about to bare my soul and tell this second star chamber (my first being Baylor's External Review Committee) what I really thought. I therefore finessed it. You can read the statement online, especially paragraph three, where I said just enough to keep my job, and just enough to give me room to recant, as I'm doing here.

If I had been feeling less vulnerable, if I had independent financial means, I would have said goodbye to Southwestern Baptist Theological Seminary right then and there. This is one of the things I find most destructive about fundamentalism, the constant threat that at any moment one can run a foul of the orthodoxy *du jour*, and be thrown under the bus because that's the proper place for heretics.

This is a deeply unhealthy situation for theological education, leading to a slavish mentality among faculty, who must constantly monitor and censor themselves if they are to stay in the good graces of the fundamentalist power structures. Upton Sinclair once remarked, "It is difficult to get a man to understand something when his salary depends upon his not understanding it." In my own case, I would amend this to, "It is difficult to get a man to candidly admit his actual beliefs when his salary depends on not admitting them."

I was always up front with Southwestern Seminary about my old-earth views. But over time it became clear that I was increasingly in the minority and that the young-earth position was the safer one to assume. Ironically, I had not misrepresented my views on Noah's flood when I was hired at Southwestern Seminary— its imply didn't come up. Indeed, the Baptist Faith & Message 2000, to which I had to subscribe, makes no mention of Noah's flood, nor was I ever asked about it during my job interview and hiring process.

In any case, outsiders saw clearly what was happening. The clearest was perhaps Andrea Bottaro, a biologist critic of intelligent design, who cut through this charade. At the Panda's Thumb blog, here marked,

> Dembski said he is an inerrantist, not a literalist. I am not really up to speed with fundie systematics, but I think that is a fairly significant difference (to them, at least).
>
> Also, I am pretty sure Dembski had to be an inerrantist (or profess to be) in order to be hired to teach in any Baptist seminary, so I think

> the big news, if any, is basically that Dembski explicitly stated that at this time he actually believes in Noah's ark myth as it is described in the Bible. It's a silly belief, and his groveling for forgiveness should be brought up any time the IDists whine about academic freedom, but it still doesn't make him a YEC [= young-earth creationism, WmAD].
>
> Dembski's book (reportedly—I have not read it) states that he believes that the evidence for an old earth is strong and that this evidence is compatible with an inerrantist interpretation of Genesis. Although he oh-hums on the topic in his recantation [i.e., my four paragraphs in the White Paper, WmAD], he has not recanted it, and that alone rules him out as a YEC. In fact, strictly speaking his current recantation also leaves him open to later recant the recantation itself, because what he actually says says is that the Bible "**seem[s]** clearly to teach" the historicity of the flood myth, pending his "exegetical, historical and theological" (and pointedly, not "scientific") work on the topic.

As much as I hate to admit it, Bottaro got it exactly right. I would still regard myself as an inerrantist, but an inerrancy in what the Bible actually teaches, not an inerrancy in what a reflexive literalism would demand of the Bible. Have I, as Bottaro suggests, left myself open to recanting the recantation? I have. Without the threat of losing my job, I see Noah's flood as a story with a theological purpose based on the historical occurrence of a local flood in the ancient Near East.

To date, I have not done the exegetical, historical, and theological work that I said I needed to do if I were weighing in on this topic again. But I'm not weighing in on this topic as a theologian or exegete or historian intent on making a rigorous argument. Having left seminary teaching for good, I'm now a private citizen entitled to my opinion.

Secular Teleology

JB: Let's return to the "problem of good," but from a different vantage. We understand why you raise this as a problem for atheists who are physicalists, reductionists, Darwinists, and others who deny the existence of either purpose or value in any objective sense. Let us call such people "metaphysical naturalists"—they look to the natural sciences, rather than our everyday experience, to tell us what exists. However, all non-theists are not metaphysical naturalists. What would you say to someone—like Aristotle, G.E. Moore, Max Scheler, Maurice Merleau-Ponty, Hans Jonas, or Thomas Nagel—who is not a traditional theist, but nevertheless believes, on the basis of common sense and introspection, that purpose and value are inherent properties of our universe?

BD: I would say, "We're on the same page when it comes to purpose and value being objective. Now let's examine their ultimate source." It seems to me that Christian theism gives a better account of these, and I would argue as such. I would bring in intelligent design and I would bring in historical evidence for the truth of Christianity. Not surprisingly, I feel much more commonality with Aristotle *et al.* than with the metaphysical naturalists.

Suboptimality of Design

JB: How do you explain suboptimal or bad design? Do you have a scientific explanation for such instances of design?

BD: The reason we put the adjective "intelligent" in front of the noun "design" is not to stress that the design we find in nature is optimal or good or morally acceptable. Rather, it is to underscore that the design we find in biology and in the universe more generally is actual. Richard Dawkins opens his book *The Blind Watchmaker* by stating "Biology is the study of complicated things that give the appearance of having been designed for a purpose."

For Darwinian biologists, all such design is merely an appearance. The "intelligent" in "intelligent design" underscores that we're not just dealing with an appearance of design, but rather with actual design.

So while the question of suboptimal or bad design may be interesting, it is not central to intelligent design as a scientific program, which in the first instance is interested in looking for evidence of design überhaupt. That said, it will be helpful to bring some clarifications to this discussion, especially since the problem of bad, and even malevolent design, is such a stumbling block for many people in accepting ID.

First off, let's be clear that design is rarely, if ever, optimal. The problem is that all designs involve compromise among competing objectives. They are multi criteria optimization problems, and the problem with multiple criteria is that there is no unique way to rank criteria.

Take a coat hanger. What is the best coat hanger? One that is strong, resilient, and extremely light. Okay, try a titanium coat hanger. But now you're paying a lot of money for the coat hanger. If one of your criteria is optimality of cost, then you'll probably forgo titanium and go with the plastic Walmart specials.

Leaving aside the issue of multicriteria optimization, one might still point to certain biological systems and argue that they could have been designed better. But I've never found such arguments clear or persuasive. One Darwinian favorite is the inverted retina of vertebrates. The wiring is backward, and any self-respecting designer, we are told, would have designed it differently.

Whenever I hear such criticisms, however, what I don't hear is a concrete redesign plan that, when implemented, actually demonstrates the superiority of the new design. It's one thing to speculate about how to make something better. It's another thing to actually do it. Evolutionary biologists are notorious for mounting arguments from imagination, where it's enough to imagine some improvement without actually implementing it. And for them, such an argument always trumps design.

With the inverted retina, there are actually good functional reasons for it. I recount that in my book *The Design of Life*, coauthored with Jonathan Wells (Foundation for Thought and Ethics, 2007). Briefly, a visual system needs three things: speed, acuity, and sensitivity. To achieve sensitivity, retinal cells need a copious blood flow. Putting nerves and blood vessels in front of the light sensitive cells allows for just that. Nor does this block light, because Müller glial cells serve asfiberoptics that bring the light without distortion to where it needs to be.

Okay, what about parasites and nasty critters that inflict pain on others? Even here, one finds that the designs are quite remarkable—the parasites seem designed to exploit their hosts. Yes, but what sort of designer would have done this? Read my book, *The End of Christianity*. Natural evil is a problem, but it is a problem for theology and not for intelligent design *per se*.

Dembski's Conception of Intelligent Design and Evolution

JB: Next, we would like to press you a bit on your conception of ID. First, let's agree to some terminological conventions, which will allow us to pose our questions more precisely. Let us call the claim that present-day life forms have descended from ancient life forms the "common-descent hypothesis," and the claim that the neo-Darwinian theory of natural selection adequately explains common descent, the "selection-mechanism thesis." Our first question, then, is this: What degree of epistemic warrant would you ascribe to the common-descent hypothesis? What degree to the selection-mechanism thesis? What are the main biological observations of complexity that the selection-mechanism thesis is simply unable to answer or explain?

BD: Common descent seems to me not all that well established. Certain fossil and molecular evidence suggests that a fair amount of evolution may have taken place (perhaps to the level of families, orders, or even classes), but the grand picture of evolution ("monad to Man," as it's been called) seems to me unsupported. Indeed, the evidence seems to be against it. Illustra Media has an interesting video titled Darwin's Dilemma, focusing on the Cambrian explosion, which challenged Darwin's theory back in his day and continues to do so today. Jonathan Wells and I devote a chapter to this in our book, *The Design of Life*.

My skepticism about common descent is not universally shared in the ID community. Michael Behe, for instance, holds to the common-descent hypothesis. But that has not resulted in any rift between him and me. We are both convinced that the selection-mechanism thesis fails. For the sake of argument, I'll often allow that common descent may be true, even though I personally reject it. But the ID community is convinced that the selection-mechanism thesis is not just unwarranted, but ascertainably false.

In saying this, we are not denying that natural selection operates. Indeed, it does. But we are denying that its range and power are anything like what the Darwinists claim. And the evidence, we would contend, is all on our side. This is probably not the place to rehearse such arguments. I refer readers to *The Design of Life*. I would also refer readers to an article I coauthored with Bob Marks entitled "Life's Conservation Law: Why Darwinian Evolution Cannot Create Biological Information." This paper can be found in *The Nature of Nature* anthology, cited earlier.

As for the types of systems that the selection-mechanism thesis is unable to account for, I would point to their reducibly complex systems to which Michael Behe first drew our attention, but with a twist. Many of the systems that Michael Behe examined in *Darwin's Black Box* (Free Press, 1996) are dispensable to life in the sense that organisms can be alive without them. Nonetheless, some systems, such as the protein synthesis apparatus, are not just irreducibly complex, but also indispensable to life.

This strengthens Behe's argument for the unevolvability of these systems, because simplifying them does not merely render unrecoverable their function, but also precludes life as such—and if you're not alive, you're not evolving. The loophole that Behe's critics have always cited against him is that irreducibly complex systems might evolve from simpler systems with different structures and functions. Thus, the function of the irreducibly complex system in question would have to be acquired later in the game. But if the function is indispensable, this loophole is closed.

Think of the bacterial flagellum. It is irreducibly complex, yes, but it is also dispensable in the sense that bacteria can get by without this motility device. But protein synthesis, which is irreducibly complex, is also indispensable. Evolve into it from something that can't perform protein synthesis, and you're dead.

JB: One way of looking at ID, overall, is as a pairing of two very different kinds of claims. On the one hand, there is the negative claim that the selection-mechanism thesis is false—that the theory of natural selection is wholly inadequate as an explanation of the fantastically complex structure and function of living things. The reason is that the proposed selection mechanism simply lacks the conceptual resources to "save the phenomena." On the other hand, ID, as usually construed, makes a positive claim, which is an inference from the appearance of design in living systems—together with the impotence of the selection mechanism to explain it—to the conclusion that design has actually been imposed on living matter by an external agent (call this the "external-design thesis").

It seems that these two claims have very different degrees of warrant. Without getting into details, it just seems inherently more plausible that the selection-mechanism thesis is false than it does that the external-design thesis is true. For one thing, lots of scientists agree with the negative thesis, but very few of them agree with the positive one. Could you please comment on this way of understanding ID, and respond to our concern about the epistemic status of its negative and positive claims?

Simply put, why would the inability of a reductionist biology to explain certain examples of biological complexity leave us solely with the conclusion of an external designer (who for most people is God)?

BD: In answering this question, let's put the selection-mechanism thesis safely to one side as either false or unjustified. Darwinists will of course demur, but a growing body of biologists who are not favorable to ID would, as you note, agree. I'm thinking especially of biologists like James Shapiro at the University of Chicago, whose *Evolution: A View from the 21st Century* (F T Press, 2011) is as thorough a dismantling of the selection-mechanism thesis as one will find.

The question, then, is: What replaces it? I would agree that the set-theoretic complement to the selection-mechanism thesis is broader than the external-design thesis, which holds that a designing intelligence operating outside ordinary natural processes was required to build organismal complexity. That said, I don't see ID as coextensive with the external-design thesis. I've argued this in my books *No Free Lunch* and *The Design Revolution*, but let recap my argumen there. "Design" can be a confusing word in these discussions because historically it has been put in opposition to nature. Things can achieve their form or structure because it is in their nature to do so—thus, they do it internally, as when an acorn grows into an oak tree. On the other hand, things can achieve their form or structure because an external efficient cause acts to bring it about, as when pieces of wood require an external technological agent to form a ship. This distinction goes back at least to Aristotle, who thus contrasted *phusis* (nature) with *techne* (which we translate "design," but is also the word from which we get "technology").

Now, my point in *No Free Lunch*, *The Design Revolution*, and elsewhere is that ID need not be identified with the design-side of this Aristotelian distinction. And the reason I give is that the materialists have confused the nature-side of this Aristotelian distinction.

If nature is understood in materialist and reductionist terms, as is common these days, then we have a far more impoverished view of nature than the ancients had.

Moreover, if we treat design as the set-theoretic complement of this impoverished view of nature, then we really have a much broader concept of design, one that certainly encompasses the external-designer view, but one that also allows for an internalist or immanent teleology. ID, as I've argued, is compatible with either of these approaches. What distinguishes ID is the detectability of design *qua* real teleology in nature. The precise nature of that teleology is logically downstream.

Personally, I think an externalist teleology works better, at least with some aspects of living systems (I have a hard time, for instance, seeing how an internalist teleology works at the level of inorganic chemicals leading up to first life). But the fundamental issue is teleology. And it does seem to me that if you reject the selection-mechanism thesis, then you will be stuck with some form of teleology.

Self-Organization and Its Discontents

JB: Setting aside issues concerning the identity of the external designer, there are an increasing number of scientists—such as, for example, Stuart Kauffman, Terrence Deacon, Mae-Wan Ho, Lenny Moss, Alberto Moreno, Ezequiel di Paolo, and others—who might accept ID's negative rejection of the Darwinists' selection-mechanism thesis, and yet deny ID's positive inference to an external designer as not logically forced upon us. The reason is that, in their view, ID overlooks a third possibility, namely, that life is an inherent attribute of a certain special condensed state—sometimes referred to as the "living state"—of matter. On this hypothesis, what looks to us like externally imposed design is really the result of an active adaptive capacity founded in the physics of living matter. Can you comment on this possibility?

BD: I allow for that possibility in my answer to the last question. But my worry is with the character of the proposals made by these scientists. I know Kauffman, Ho, and Moss's work best, and it seems to me that they don't really give you a robust teleology. Rather, there is a minimalist natural teleology (such as condensation or vaguely articulated adaptive capacities), which then magically gets boot strapped to things like butterflies.

I've always found such self-organizational scenarios unsatisfying, because, to my mind, they don't really solve anything. Now you might say, how does design solve anything? Well, we know that designers can build some amazing things, like Lear Jets. And so, when we see a butterfly, which is far more marvelous than a Lear Jet, we are extrapolating—reasonably in my view—from the characteristics of designers and design processes that we know. But I don't see any way to extrapolate reasonably from condensation or criticality or convective processes to butterflies.

Alternate Approaches to Specified Complexity

JB: David L. Abel's book, *The First Gene* (Long View Press—Academic, 2011), takes aim at "self-organization" theories of the type mentioned in the previous question. We believe the publication of this book is likely to be a watershed event. Have you read it yet? What do you see as the relation between your work and his?

BD: I've dipped into the book and am familiar with some of the earlier work by Abel on which it is based. So, even though I haven't read the 500-plus pages that make up this book word-for-word, I think I have a pretty good idea of its content. I'm afraid I don't share your optimistic view of the book. Which is not to say that I'm unsympathetic with its point of view or many of the arguments it's making. I just don't see anything all that original there in terms of fundamental theory, nor do I think it is presenting the most powerful information-theoretic case for real teleology in nature.

I've known Abel since 1998. He was back then heading up the Gene Emergence Project, which offered a multimillion-dollar Origin of Life Prize to the first person to make a convincing argument for how life might have emerged by naturalistic means. Abel took this tack on strategic grounds, thinking that it's easier and wiser to defeat Darwinian naturalism not by demonstrating design but by demonstrating the repeated failure of naturalistic processes to bring about life. In fact, at the time, he wouldn't have anything public to do with me or my ID colleagues because he wanted to maintain his credibility within the scientific community at large.

In any case, I'm entirely with him that self-organizational scenarios, as they are typically characterized—in that they exclude real teleology—don't work. But his preferred construct for analyzing such scenarios and making the case for teleology—something he calls "prescriptive information"—strikes me as too fuzzy and qualitative to serve as a powerful analytic tool.

In fact, insofar as this notion can be made rigorous (which Abel never seems to do in his book), it seems that it would be a special case of my own specified complexity. Specified complexity—or "complex specified information" (as I've also called it), and especially its most recent incarnation in the form of "active information"—seems to me in a better position to accomplish what Abel wants.

But let readers decide for themselves. Having read his book, let them check out my publication sat the EvolutionaryInformaticsLab.

The Concept of Information

JB: As your last answer makes clear, one of the key concepts you use in your work on ID is "information." We have two questions about this. First, it seems to us that information, properly speaking, is always information-for-an-agent. That is, there is no such thing, strictly speaking, as information in the abstract, unrelated to some agent or intelligence for which the information is meaningful. So-called information, abstracted from its meaning for an agent, is really more properly termed "structure" or "pattern" or something of that sort. Given this definitional stipulation, then, the way the ID literature relies upon the concept of information appears question-begging, at least with respect to its positive claim—the external-design thesis. That is to say, ID's inference to an external designer seems to depend upon a premise about information that already tacitly assumes the existence of an intelligence external to all living matter. Would you care to comment?

BD: I'm afraid I don't agree with your first premise here. Whenever I set the groundwork for information in a discussion of ID, I make clear that information happens when there is a reduction of possibilities. Initially, there is a range of live possibilities. Later, one of these possibilities is realized. Information happens in that reduction and realization.

Now, the individuation of these possibilities and the causal process involved in their realization need involve no external intelligence. Tomorrow, it may rain or it may not rain. Both are live possibilities, and the fact that they are live possibilities does not depend on my, or any other external intelligence, drawing the distinction between rain and no rain. Moreover, the causal processes responsible for rain do not presuppose an external intelligence (at least not obviously so, though one might argue that if God created the world and providentially guides it, intelligence is involved even in the rain that falls).

So, in answer to your question, nature can produce information and in doing so it need beg no questions about external designers. That said, external designers can also produce information—as I am doing now by typing out my answer to your question. What makes the design inference work is a coincidence between information produced by nature and information produced by designers.

We see such a coincidence, for instance, in the bacterial flagellum. Ostensibly, nature produced it. And yet humans, as designing agents and without knowledge of such systems, also produced bidirectional motor-driven propellers. This coincidence calls for explanation, especially when it is cashed out with the full probabilistic design-theoretic apparatus that I develop. But the bottom line, in answer to your question, is that information, properly construed, is a powerful notion that need not presuppose an agent or semantics in the way you suggest. There is thus no begging of the question.

JB: Here is our other question regarding information. There are quite a few physicists out there—of whom John Archibald Wheeler is perhaps the best known—who regard information as a primitive concept, meaning that the entity to which the term refers is on an ontological par with matter and energy, or particles and fields, or whatever else one takes to be the absolutely basic building blocks of the universe. Do you agree with this? If you do, how do you feel about the company you are keeping? If you don't, then what sort of more synthetic account would you give of information?

BD: Yes, I remember reading in Wheeler's biography that he had his particle stage (everything is particles), then his fields stage (everything is fields), and then his information stage (everything is information). I remember Stanford's Keith Devlin also making a similar point several decades ago about information possibly being a fundamental entity (he subsequently backed away from this).

I would agree that information is a fundamental entity and am happy to put myself in this company. Perhaps it's easier to take this view now a days than in previous generations. We are a wash with information. This is an information age.

Moreover, we all know about information going through multiple transformations and embodiments.

When you send an email, your fingers type at a keyboard, producing ASCII or UTF-8 or some other encoded text. This is then transformed into some other symbol string so that it can be moved across the Internet without error (using error-correcting codes). Then, that information needs to be reconstituted at the other end.

The same sorts of processes are going on in life. Information is transmitted from DNA to RNA to amino-acid sequences. It's not just that we see alpha numeric-type items arranged sequentially in biology, but that we see transformation from one such sequence to another. Although it no longer surprises us, it should surprise us that there is such a thing as a genetic CODE.

Think about it—to code something is to take a character string in one form and transform it into another character string, where it can be useful in a way it wasn't before the transformation. Alan Turing, Claude Shannon, and others were dealing with and developing the mathematics for such codes in the 1940s, and then, lo, in the 1950s we find that such codes are in all our cells. This is remarkable.

I think we're just scratching the surface of information in nature. I've got a massive, one-volume encyclopedia of physics on my shelf with publication date 1992. Neither among the main entries nor in the extensive index does the word "information" appear. Since then, it's been gaining momentum. I predict that information will play an increasingly dominant role throughout the natural sciences in coming years.

What Would an ID Curriculum Look Like?

JB: What would a school lesson plan of ID consist of? How many lessons or hours would be required to study and understand the theory? Would it fill entire semesters for students? What body of research would such a curriculum cite? Is there a substantial literature of ID papers in the peer-reviewed science journals that could be cited?

BD: ID theorists, in developing their views about design in nature, appeal to the full range of mathematical, engineering, biological, and physical sciences. So an ID curriculum will include everything their Darwinian counterparts are currently studying. But there will be more. I can think of ten full-semester college courses off the top of my head that would have significant ID content and could not reasonably be taught from a Darwinian perspective:

1. Evolvability and Unevolvability (biology)
2. Conservation of Information Theorems (mathematics)
3. Bayesian and Fisherian Design Inferences (statistics)
4. The Failure of Naturalistic Origin of Life Scenarios (chemistry)

5   Toward a Nonreductive Neuroscience (psychology/neuroscience)
6   Recovering Free Will (philosophy of mind)
7   Ethics, Biology, and Responsibility (ethics)
8   The Comprehensible Universe (cosmology)
9   The Unreasonable Effectiveness of Mathematics (philosophy of mathematics)
10 The Reductionist Roots of Modern Science (history and philosophy of science)

One thing to understand: ID looks at the very same data that Darwinists are looking at. As Nobelist Lawrence Bragg remarked, "The important thing in science is not so much to obtain new facts as to discover new ways of thinking about them." ID is thinking about the world in new ways. So, one way for ID to get into a lesson plan is simply for textbooks to be rewritten from an ID perspective.

For instance, a standard basal biology textbook will have many facts about biology, but it will also frame those facts within a Darwinian picture of the world. Some of the more recent textbooks will even slam ID. Such a textbook could be rewritten, giving the standard evolutionary accounts, but also critiquing them and indicating the lines of evidence that argue for a design conclusion.

Theodosius Dobzhansky is famously quoted as saying that "nothing in biology makes sense except in the light of evolution," by which he meant the neo-Darwinian theory of evolution. From the ID perspective, life is replete with the marks of intelligence, an intelligence not reducible to Darwinian processes. Perhaps the biggest part that ID will play in most curricula for now, leaving aside courses that deal with its specific contributions in the peer-reviewed literature, is in framing the various disciplines and fields that have been infected with Darwinian thinking.

As for the ID peer-reviewed literature, I wouldn't say it's substantial, but it is growing. Fifteen years ago there was almost nothing. Now there's a fair amount, as can be seen at the Evolutionary Informatics Lab, the journal Bio-Complexity, and the Discovery site.

Favorite Christian Authors

JB: Who are your favorite Christian or other theist authors? (We define "theism" as belief in a God who created and sustains the world in existence, and who cares about particular human beings.) Which books would you especially recommend to people who would like to learn more about Christianity and/or theism?

BD: G. K. Chesterton's *Orthodoxy* and C. S. Lewis' *Miracles* are high on my list. As for learning more about Christianity and theism, I strongly encourage reading the Bible, though without literalist or modernist presuppositions. I tend to prefer the Church fathers over Reformation and post-Renaissance theologians, especially as exemplified in the classic anthology of Eastern Orthodox spiritual writings called the *Philokalia*.

I've tended to read in phases. Early in my Christian walk, I found the writings of Francis Schaeffer helpful. Inretrospect, I don't think his scholarship was all that great, but in the 1970s and 80s, he urged evangelical Christians to undertake a rigorous intellectual examination of the faith at a time when most of the "smart people" talking about Christianity had capitulated to modernism/liberalism and no longer had anything that resembled traditional Christianity.

For some years I was especially taken with Christian apologetics. I had a phase reading John Warwick Montgomery, whose Festschrift, titled *Toughminded Christianity*, I ended up co-editing. Montgomery in the 1960s was a lone ranger, taking on the "God is dead" theologians with flair and attitude. Somewhere in the 1970s, however, I think he got side tracked, trying wear too many hats (attorney, theologian, historian, archaeologist, etc.). But it's likely that apologists like Bill Craig, Robert Newman, John Bloom, and me would not have gotten multiple doctorates and devoted ourselves to apologetics without his example.

Another reading phase that deeply influenced me, especially in underscoring the importance of embracing a non-Kantian metaphysical realism, focused on jointly studying Stanley Jaki and Etienne Gilson. Though I never got fully on board with their Thomism (my sensibilities are more with the common sense realism of Thomas Reid), I think they got it right that the crisis in modern philosophy is a crisis of metaphysics. My book *Being as Communion* takes this tack.

Other Christian titles that I've enjoyed are Diogenes Allen's *Spiritual Theology*, Alexander Schmemann's *For the Life of the World*, and Tom Oden's three volume theology as well as his Ancient Christian Commentary on Scripture (which culls from the writings of the Church Fathers their collective commentary on all of Scripture).

Older titles that I would recommend include Boethius's *Consolation of Philosophy*, Epictetus's *Enchiridion* (Stoic philosophy at its best — much better than Marcus Aurelius's *Meditations*, which strikes me as cold and detached), and Maimonides's *Guide for the Perplexed*. Maimonides had an impressive intellect. Epictetus and Maimonides were, of course, non-Christians, but I find their work nonetheless inspiring.

Favorite Atheist Authors

JB: Are there any atheist authors whom you enjoy reading or whose work you respect? Are there any philosophical critics of Christianity and/or theism whose work you have found challenging?

BD: I've read many of Christianity's critics, but I can't say I've ever had the reaction, "That really throws me for a loop. Now I've got to rethink my faith in God." I've enjoyed reading some atheist authors more as entertainment and cultural commentary (e.g., Bertrand Russell and Christopher Hitchens), but I can't say I was all that impressed with their arguments. Moreover, professional analytic philosophy in general leaves me cold, so its atheist practitioners who apply their methods to dismantling theism leave me doubly cold.

Sorry I can't be more of help here, or for that matter on the last question. The type of reading I enjoy most and that stimulates me most takes one of two forms: (1) biographical and historical writing that focuses on interesting personalities, events, and stories; and (2) writing that attempts to understand and resolve difficult problems, in which challenging questions receive ingenious solutions. In brief, I enjoy history and biography, and I remain a mathematician at heart.

Converts to Intelligent Design

JB: Has ID turned many atheists into theists or merely satisfied theists' existing beliefs? What is the apologetic value of ID?

BD: I have plenty of anecdotal evidence for the power of intelligent design to shake atheists out of their dogmatic slumbers and bring them to theism. Indeed, by email and at lectures, I encounter people who claim that my own work on ID has played that role. But it would be interesting to have Barna or Gallup do a professional survey in which ID's role as a corrective to atheism could more accurately be gauged.

As for the apologetic value of ID, I see it mainly as a ground-clearing operation, getting rid of the obstacles that naturalism has placed in the way of people coming to take the possibility of God as a live option. A reductive Darwinian science has, in my experience, been one of the main obstacles to belief in God, at least in Western culture. Hitchens, Dawkins, and Dennett have all looked to Darwin as their patron saint, giving them his blessing to repudiate theism. Dawkins even wrote that Darwin made it possible to be an intellectually fulfilled atheist.

So, if we think of atheism as a cultural phenomenon that looks to science for backing and if we think of ID as undoing that backing and thus making theism that much more plausible, we have an apologetic rationale for ID.

Recommended Colleges

JB: If you had to guide a college-bound high school senior on where to pursue undergraduate studies, what would you say? What are some of the top schools and programs that embody your educational philosophy? Where would you not send this high school senior?

BD: A non-negotiable for me with any college I would recommend is that it put a premium on freedom of thought and expression, steering clear of the political correctness, affirmative action, and ideological pressure that infects so much of higher education. Without such freedom, education, in my view, degenerates into indoctrination, creating not people who can think for themselves but pawns of powerful interests.

A school that has taken the lead in advancing academic freedom is my alma mater, the University of Chicago, whose Committee on Freedom of Expression has articulated a policy statement known as the "Chicago Statement". As of August 30, 2019, almost 70 schools signed the statement, including Princeton, Purdue, and Vanderbilt.

As a Christian, I would like to recommend Christians colleges, but for me to do so in good conscience, such schools need to be Christian in more than just name. Indeed, I'm dead-set against many so-called Christian colleges that use their public Christian identity to mask a secular agenda. Many Christian institutions have an inferiority complex in which they're trying to ape the secular academy to gain its approval. Those that resist this mentality often adopt a fundamentalist mind set in which they pretend they've got the answer to every important question nailed down. That may work in a Christian ghetto, but it has no traction in the wider culture.

I'm painting with a broad brush, and individual faculty at these institutions will vary, and some of them will be very fine. The challenge with Christian education is to steer clear of progressivism/liberalism on the one hand (which explicitly denies the faith) and likewise to steer clear of fundamentalism/dogmatism on the other hand (which neutralizes the faith in the wider culture).

Given these provisos, I would say the following Christian institutions seem quite promising: Grove City College, Biola University, Union University, Dordt University, Northwestern College (MN), Taylor University, Oral Roberts University, Houston Baptist University, and The King's College (in New York City). These are just off the top of my head—back in the day I spoke at several of these schools about intelligent design. There are, I'm sure, some (but not too many) others.

Leaving aside Christian education, my first impulse in advising Christian parents on where to send their high schoolers is to recommend an academically solid private or state school at which there is a healthy Christian community on/near campus that will keep them on the straight and narrow as they face the temptations of college life. At least one good local church is vital for such a community, and some outspoken Christian faculty are a bonus.

Where would I not send such high schoolers? To campuses with a flaming progressive agenda that delights in exposing students to the perversity and decadence of our culture. Schools that offer freshman seminars in body piercing or sex reassignment surgery or queer studies would, for me, be off the table.

Word of advice to parents: Don't just look at the brochures and catalogs that schools send out and don't just go where the tour guides take you on your campus visit. Look at the course schedule for a semester and see what's being offered to incoming freshmen. Sit in on some classes. Sit in on highly publicized lectures. Look at bulletin boards and see what campus groups are prominent (is it the local InterVarsity chapter of the local LGBTQ caucus?). Go to the campus bookstore and see what texts students are reading. Go to the student center, eat in the cafeteria, and get a sense of the campus culture first-hand. If it leaves you feeling queasy, move onto another school.

Dealing with Rejection

JB: We are curious to know what it was like, on a personal level, to be on the receiving end of so much scorn and vituperation over the years—to be a human lightning rod, so to speak. How did it feel? Were you surprised by what happened to you? . . . angered? . . . disappointed? How were you able to cope? What got you through the toughest times?

BD: An answer to this question needs to start with some perspective and sense of proportion. I've had a regular income all these years, been able to care for my family, been able to do my research, had minimal teaching, gotten lots of books published, and I now find myself with the respect of a small but committed community. This is not persecution on the scale of the former Eastern Bloc, where being demoted as a professor meant working as a janitor or being sent off to the Gulag.

So, a lot of people are unhappy with me. Who cares? By and large, not me. I'm not interested in reading the abuse that was regularly leveled against me (it's actually a lot less now that I've turned from ID to education). The marginalization and ostracism that I experienced, at Baylor and later from fundamentalists, has been harder to deal with.

But I've always felt that the best way to respond to enemies is by being productive and not allowing them to distract me. This has helped. Sure, I haven't followed my own advice perfectly. And I've taken some bruising. But it is really nothing compared to what Christians persecuted for their faith have endured over history and endure even to this day. This perspective steadies me.

Another thing that has put things in perspective for me is the autism of my son John. My good wife and I have been dealing with this for well over fifteen years now. We are still working on getting him well, but there's a lot that has to change for that to happen. My son is now 18, not fully potty trained, needs to be showered and dressed, and still doesn't speak. I've never had a conversation with him and don't know if I ever will, this side of eternity.

Because of my son's plight—and it is a plight; he's not happy being autistic, dealing with constant sensory overload and the a praxia, aphasia, etc. that are part of his condition—I've lost all enthusiasm for engaging in ego contests with critics. I used to do this, but much less so now (and hopefully not at all). My interest these days is taking care of my family and being productive without strife or distraction.

Retooling and Focusing on Education

JB: In the last few years, you've shifted your focus from intelligent design to education. Talk to us about that. Would it be fair to say that you have "left" intelligent design? Why have you turned to education? What are you doing in that regard?

BD: I'm happy with the work I've done on intelligent design and repudiate none of it. But after twenty-five years working in this area, I felt I needed a break. Also, I've wearied of the isolation and controversy that continually dogged my work on intelligent design.

So I turned to business—the business of education, which is a big business. I've been able to earn a good income developing educational content, products, and software. A lot of this work is still in start-up mode, so I don't want to say too much at this time.

My book on the life and work of high school math teacher Jaime Escalante (*It Takes Ganas: Jaime Escalante's Secret toInspired Learning*, co authored with Alex Thomas) exemplifies my educational philosophy. I'm deeply interested in making education far more effective than it is now, especially with the use of innovative technologies, and in providing free education to the majority or developing world at the K-12 level.

I'm working closely with a start up to gamify education. I think we waste a tremendous amount of time and resources in education, so I'm hoping to play a positive role in effectively delivering educational content, especially to provide the knowledge and skills people need to do satisfying work and adequately support their families.

My motto in all this educational work is the statement by Stoic philosopher Epictetus "Only the educated are free."

Final Thoughts

JB: Any final thoughts you would like to share with our readers? What do you see as the chances that free and open debate, without intimidation, about natural selection and evolution will be possible in this country anytime soon? Where do you hope to be personally 5 years from now? What does the future hold for the ID movement? Where would you like see it stand in coming generations?

BD: The epigraph to my book *The Design Revolution* is a quote from a short essay of Pascal's called the "The Art of Persuasion": "People almost invariably arrive at their beliefs not on the basis of proof but on the basis of what they find attractive." When I got into ID in the early 1990s, I thought truth and its validation (what Pascal calls "proof") was enough, or at least close to enough. Now that I'm older and wiser, I see that the majority of people have other priorities. Even those who protest that they love truth (Richard Dawkins is one) will use such protestations to advance their own biases and agendas. Here, I'm addressing myself as well—certainly earlier in my career, selfish ambition and narcissism were vying furiously in my so-called" quest for truth." Perhaps I've not put these aside yet.

I've found self-deception as much among Christians as among atheists and agnostics. In fact, I've come to like dealing with secularists better than with Christians who use religion as a cloak to cover their pride and absence of love. Secularists are at least more likely to admit that they're being bad. Christians, especially American evangelical Christians, with pietism in the background, have to pretend to be good.

What does all this have to do with your question? It's this: Whereas in my past life I was all gung-ho about ID becoming the new reigning paradigm that would replace conventional evolutionary theory, I no longer have that optimism. That's not to say I'm not going to continue to work toward that end. I will. And I could see ID's fortunes changing quickly. But I could also see the old paradigm lingering on. The former Soviet Union collapsed very quickly even though it looked invincible a few years earlier. Our banking system, by contrast, has been skirting insolvency for decades and continually seems able to kick the can down the road. ID, in my view, has the better argument. But as an attorney sitting across his desk from a client put it in a *New Yorker* cartoon dating back more than 60 years: "You have a pretty good case, Mr. Pitkin. How much justice can you afford?" I'm not sure how much justice ID can afford.

Despite all the publicity it's gotten, it has few backers. Atheistic evolutionists hate it. Theistic evolutionists hate it. And fundamentalists have lost most of their enthusiasm for it because it doesn't deliver the pat answers about creation that they had hoped for.

Machiavelli had an insight that's relevant here:

> "It must be considered that there is nothing more difficult to carry out nor more doubtful of success, nor more dangerous to handle, than to initiate a new order of things. For the reformer has enemies in all those who profit by the old order, and only lukewarm defenders in all those who would profit by the new order, this lukewarmness arising partly for fear of their adversaries,who have the laws in their favor; and partly from the incredulity of men,who do not truly believe in anything new until they have had actual experience of it" [*The Prince*, Chapter Six—ed.].

With this preamble, let me answer your questions directly: I don't see free and open debate regarding evolution coming anytime soon—not until the Darwinists, kicking and dragging, are forced to acknowledge that there is a problem with their view. This may happen with another court case (the *Dover* case was a loss for ID, but it did not go to the Supreme Court; so, I could see another case reversing *Dover*).

That said, I put very little stock in court cases. Eventually, the evidence for ID will disseminate widely enough so that Darwinists will not be able to stifle the conversation. For now, however, they can. I think of a story told to me by one Baylor student (this happened after I left): Biology students wanting to do a summer research internship in the Biology Department are quizzed regarding their views on ID. If they are perceived as sympathetic to it, they are denied the research opportunity. For now, that's how the game is played, and ID is kept at bay.

Five years from now, I expect still to be dipping back into ID occasionally, but I expect to be spending the bulk of my time, as now, developing educational content, curriculum, and technologies. I also expect to branch out into economics and developing social technologies. I have some ideas about developing a strongly encrypted, decentralized, information-based form of money that cannot be proliferated at will, as are our present fiat currencies, but also doesn't succumb to the limitations of peer-to-peer distributed networks and blockchains such as bitcoin. I've written a long white paper on this, but the proposal still needs some work. If it can be made to work, I'd like to disseminate such a monetary system as well as other social technologies as a way of advancing human freedom.

It seems to me that the greatest challenge to our freedoms—a challenge I see all the time in the ID debate—is the centralization of power. I see my coming years as an effort to unseat these monopolies. I realize this may sound grandiose, but we live in a technocratic age in which the elite think they know what's best for us—and they do not, the evidence of which is staring us in the face.

Ultimately, I think ID will win. When I was in my 40s, I thought I'd be around to see its victory. Now that I'm close to 60, I'm not so sure. The Bible comforts me in this regard, because one sees in it that God's purposes are not generally carried out by the flamboyant, well-placed, and powerful. In the end, the false prophets are always clearly identified, and those who were true are vindicated. ID, in my view, plays such a prophetic role for our culture.

In the end, what I see as winning it for ID is the tendency in the long run for reality to vindicate truth. Unfortunately, as Keynes pointed out, in the long run, we're all dead. I believe the most interesting and fruitful science will in the end bed one under ID's umbrella because it gets at the truth of the matter—the intelligence that animates nature. When that happens, scientists will vote with their feet, abandoning Darwinism and embracing design. I hope to see this in my lifetime, but I'm not holding my breath.

Copyright ©2021 Bill Dembski

DEFENDING THE EMBATTLED CHRISTIAN HERITAGE OF WESTERN CIVILIZATION, CAMPION COLLEGE

Paul Morrissey

There can be no doubt in anyone's mind that we are living in extraordinary times.

As many of us have shifted to home-based lifestyles, we may find ourselves reflecting more on our lives and the world around us.

It's not just the pandemic that has changed our world so drastically; our culture is nearly unrecognisable from just a decade ago.

With the rise of identity politics influencing education, not to mention a relativistic morality pervading the fabric of our culture, one can reasonably ask: what has gone wrong with education? How can we fix it? And how can I be sure that my children are being educated and not indoctrinated?

A classical education (or "liberal arts" or "humanities") focuses on four key areas: philosophy/theology, the natural sciences, social sciences and arts. Historically, it relates to the great traditions of higher learning going back to Plato's Academy and the medieval universities (hence "classical").

Campion College, located in storied Sydney, Australia, a land which includes both European and Aboriginal culture, offers a three-year Bachelor of Arts degree that is a journey through Western Civilisation, from Ancient Greece through today, studying history, philosophy, theology, literature, and classical languages. This "Great Books"-style course of study has been used in Western education for centuries.

Opinion writer S.A. Dance once wrote, "To study the humanities is to explore nothing less than the meaning of life itself, which leads to a greater understanding of virtue and justice." In other words, a true education is one that helps form not just the mind but also one's moral judgment, furnishing a student with the ability to think, and judge, for him or herself.

More importantly, it illuminates that which transcends the material world: truth, beauty, and goodness, otherwise known as the Transcendentals.

The greatest intellectual and artistic works sprang from the pursuit of the true, the good and the beautiful. Writers such as Shakespeare, Dostoyevsky, and Austen, philosophers like Aristotle and St. Thomas Aquinas, artists like Da Vinci and such musicians as Victoria and Palestrina, not to mention moderns like Dawson, McIntyre and St. John Paul II, were all motivated by the Transcendentals. All have contributed to the formation of what we know as Western Civilisation.

And studying Western Civilisation fundamentally affects how one sees the world. You can't truly appreciate the perennial relevance of Milton's Paradise Lost without studying medieval theology and philosophy. Those who pursue law or politics approach them differently from those who haven't studied Plato or Aquinas.

Unlike the US, Australia has no long and proud tradition of the liberal arts. Campion, founded in 2006, is a pioneer — the first and the only Catholic tertiary liberal arts college in the country.

Broadly speaking, the inspiration for Campion can be traced to its contacts with similar institutions in Europe and North America, and historically, relating to the great traditions of higher learning in the liberal arts going back to the medieval universities and Plato's Academy.

More recently, however, Campion's name and origin stem from the Campion Fellowship, a national association of Catholics formed in 1973 to provide adult education programs. From the 1970s, the Campion Fellowship enjoyed strong links with Catholic liberal arts universities and colleges in America and, in time, developed a proposal to found a corresponding institution here in Australia.

Campion's founders aimed to provide a broad, pre-vocational education at the undergraduate level, based on a similar curriculum of core subjects in the humanities and sciences, but suited to Australian cultural conditions and educational requirements.

The college, like the fellowship, was named after the notable 16th century Oxford scholar and martyr, St Edmund Campion, who had long served as a patron of lay Catholic educational initiatives in Australia, beginning with the Campion Society in the 1930s.

In 2001, the Campion Foundation Limited was established as a public company to build upon this earlier work and to provide the necessary planning and financial support for the founding of Campion College Australia. The Foundation continues to operate as the college's long-term fund-raising arm, purchasing the 10-acre campus at Old Toongabbie in Western Sydney. It has recently also begun funding future building developments for the college's expansion.

On 1 July 2005, Campion College was officially approved as a registered Australian higher education institution by the NSW Department of Education and Training. The College's foundation undergraduate degree, a Bachelor of Arts in the Liberal Arts, was accredited on the same date.

The college's first staff members were gradually appointed, a substantial academic library was assembled, and a comprehensive building refurbishment was undertaken in preparation for the College's opening in 2006.

Campion's first graduation ceremony, in December 2008, was a significant milestone. It marked the first phase of the institution's development, as the inaugural students received their degrees, and it confirmed the College's commitment to nurture future students in the liberal arts who will, by the quality of their education, be able to live out a mission of leadership and service to society.

Today, Campion caters to around 140 students, with around 75 per cent of our undergraduate students living on campus. While the past 18 months have been incredibly tough for all higher education providers, we are optimistic about our growth in the near future, and have already started expanding the facilities on campus to cater to our growing demand.

In August 2018, we unveiled our first expansion to the college since its inception – two single-sex residential houses, accommodating a total of 34 students. These were built in addition to the male and female dormitories housed in the main building.

We will soon be embarking on the exciting next stage of campus development. This will include an entire new wing, housing a two-storey library, an expanded dining hall and event space, additional lecture theatres and tutorial rooms, amongst other additions. It's going to be a huge undertaking but we're so excited to see Campion expand and grow.

And it is increasingly apparent just how crucial Campion's existence is: a recent study identified it as one of only three tertiary institutions in the country that adequately taught Western history — and that Campion's course was the stand-out of the three.

Campion has a distinct Australian flavour. Occupying a former Marist seminary, the campus is filled with native Australian gum trees and wildlife. It's quite remarkable to be neck-deep in board reports, emails and essay marking, only to be interrupted by the call of kookaburras or native magpies just outside your window.

Campion's mission is to pass on the West's vast repository of knowledge, ideas, art, faith and, just as importantly, a sense of wonderment, to the next generation – and to be a corrective to the corrosive influence of identity politics infecting society. We are convinced the understanding of these things makes all the difference to our graduates, their work, their faith — and our world.

Paul Morrissey, president of Campion College since 2015, has a Licentiate in Sacred Theology from the Lateran University in Rome and his Doctorate from the Catholic Institute in Sydney.

To find out more about Campion College please consider subscribing to the free quarterly newsletter at https://www.campion.edu.au/becomeafriend/.

IN PURSUIT OF FREEDOM OF SPEECH AND ACADEMIC EXCELLENCE:

Sheridan Institute of Higher Education

By Augusto Zimmermann

The Australian Baptist Education Inc. (ABE) is the sponsoring organisation behind the establishment of the Sheridan Institute of Higher Education, in Perth, Western Australia. The Baptist Church is one of the most well-known denominations in Protestant Christianity. With regard to education, Baptists are the third largest provider of private education in Western Australia, after the Anglican and Catholic churches.

Internationally, Baptists have a rich inheritance in higher education and were involved in the establishment of a number of independent colleges in England, including founding Bristol College (1679). Several major higher education institutions in the United States also share with Sheridan a distinct Baptist heritage. The University of Chicago, Brown University and Temple University were originally founded by Baptists, and others, including Baylor University, Mercer University, and Union University, still retain a strong Baptist identity today.

Sheridan is, therefore, a higher education provider grounded in the remarkable Baptist academic tradition. Like Campion College, Avondale University and the University of Notre Dame Australia, Sheridan is also a Christian higher education provider. Sheridan's students are not required to follow the Christian faith. However, they will be introduced to the values and principles of the faith that guide Sheridan's founders.

In saying so, it is important to consider that Sheridan welcomes students and visitors of all faiths and none into its community. In contrast to secular universities that hinder the presentation of competing worldviews while denying the validity to any claim to ultimate truth, Sheridan acknowledges ultimate truths and that real differences between worldviews exist, and in doing so creates a space for genuine dialogue and engagement to take place.

The *Sheridan Statement of Academic* Freedom notes that Baptists were at the forefront of the struggle for individual rights and liberties. Baptists are traditionally driven by an unyielding commitment to the common good, which is wedded to the principles of religious liberty and freedom of conscience. They are also committed to defending the basic right of individuals to freely associate with one another on the basis of shared beliefs, and to exercise the right to dissent when those beliefs diverge.

The origin of Sheridan's commitment to academic freedom is particularly found in a fractious group of English exiles living in Amsterdam in the early 17th century. In enlightened tracts and sermons, those first Baptists were among the earliest advocates for these three foundation principles of modern democracy: freedom of conscience, freedom of speech, and freedom of association. These principles continue to have immense relevance for the 21st century, and it is in the context of its rich Baptist heritage that Sheridan affirms its commitment to the important principle of academic freedom.

All students at Sheridan study subjects that are known as the 'Common Core' units. These units are 'Introduction to Christianity', 'Survey of the Bible', and 'Christianity as a Worldview'. These units are conducted from an interdisciplinary perspective, and through the study of these units, Sheridan's students not only learn the basics of a classical education, but also gain historical, philosophical, theological, moral and ethical knowledge that is very much relevant to their undergraduate studies. In saying so, it is important to consider that Sheridan welcomes students and visitors of all faiths and none into its community.

Sheridan currently offers undergraduate programs not only in the Humanities and Social Sciences but also in Business and Science, in addition to postgraduate courses in Business Administration and Education. It is recognised for recruiting excellent academic staff and designing academic programs that deliver high quality higher education outcomes for students, engaging them in research projects which provide a unique opportunity for them to develop the skills and knowledge they need for the workplace.

Another important goal of Sheridan is to achieve academic excellence in tertiary education. To achieve this goal, academic freedom is heavily promoted and class sizes are smaller than the average class size at other universities. We place a special focus on research and practical skills, which makes us especially able to the pursuit of teaching, research, and professional development that is characterised by intellectual rigour, thorough cogent reason, and effective written and spoken persuasion.

It is an absolute honour for me to work at Sheridan. I left a tenured position at Murdoch because I have better and more exciting plans for my academic life. For example, at Murdoch I would never be allowed to hold a conference on "Religious Freedom at the Crossroads – The Rise of Anti-Christian Sentiment in Australia", simply because the university administrators are committed to cultural diversity and moral relativism. Yet, here at Sheridan I was able to organise a historical international conference on the subject, which was held in June 2019 and its keynote was a leading American constitutional lawyer and our Patron a former Prime Minister of Australia – The Hon. John Howard AM.

Of course, this problem is not restricted to one particular university. Increasingly, universities are more interested in not upsetting certain people than protecting academic freedom. The Institute of Public Affairs has carried out a systematic study of what is happening to higher education, and it found that the vast majority of Australian universities adopt policies that substantially limit freedom of speech. Such failure is seriously imperilling the discovery of truth, the core purpose of these universities.

By contrast, what is particularly attractive about Sheridan is that our academics have the freedom to exercise our professional and personal judgment in teaching and research. We are encouraged to disseminate the results of that research without undue interference from the Sheridan administration or from outside institutions and individuals. Should a complaint be made to the Institute, the administration will protect faculty from any request to retract or modify their research, publication, or teaching.

I have now been assisting Sheridan to apply for the teaching and conferral of Bachelor of Laws Degree. Sheridan's LLB pro-gram will equip students to become leaders in law with a su-perior education in conformity to a distinctively jurispruden-tial approach that will make our LLB program unique from all other law schools. This means also that our students will be prepared not only to enter the legal profession but also to make a substantial impact on our community, nation, and the world.

To conclude, Sheridan is the ideal place for students who wish not just to preserve their faith but to further enhance their knowledge of the truth. In keeping with the Baptist traditions of personal liberty and the right to dissent, our students are trained in critical thinking, taught to evaluate evidence and challenge bias (their own, their classmates, and their lecturers), to arrive at their own conclusions, and to fearlessly and respectfully argue the case for those conclusions. As such, there is no doubt in my mind that Sheridan will be gradually affirming itself as one of the finest institutions of higher education in this country.

Prof. Augusto Zimmermann PhD

Perth/WA, 20 July 2021

> Dr Augusto Zimmermann is Professor and Head of Law at Sheridan Institute of Higher Education, and Professor of Law (Adjunct) at the University of Notre Dame Australia, Sydney campus. He is also a former Law Reform Commissioner in Western Australia (2012-2017) and President of the Western Australian Legal Theory Association (WALTA).

www.ingramcontent.com/pod-product-compliance
Ingram Content Group UK Ltd.
Pitfield, Milton Keynes, MK11 3LW, UK
UKHW041409180426
11947UKWH00007B/22